Let's Destroy Alberta's Families

PASCAL RONALD

 FriesenPress

Suite 300 - 990 Fort St
Victoria, BC, V8V 3K2
Canada

www.friesenpress.com

ISBN
978-1-5255-5979-2 (Hardcover)
978-1-5255-5980-8 (Paperback)
978-1-5255-5981-5 (eBook)

1. FAMILY & RELATIONSHIPS, DYSFUNCTIONAL FAMILIES

Distributed to the trade by The Ingram Book Company

Let's Destroy Alberta's Families

An Indictment of Child and Family Services Alberta

A TRUE STORY

Table of Contents

FOREWORD

The recent media coverage of the residential schools fiascos of the early 1900s and the political attempts at reconciliation may have helped political parties seeking more votes from the electorate, but I maintain that they have done virtually nothing to help the actual victims that either died or were abused. Nor have they done anything to mend the damage caused to their families. Political correctness sells well and is for appearance only. The real damage that was caused by the trauma that the victims endured is almost impossible to erase and remains like a large scar in their brains. Without appropriate, and many times, prolonged treatment, it will haunt the victims throughout their lifetimes. Although governments claim that they have learned from their mistakes, the following true story attests to my view that they have learned very little, if nothing at all, or perhaps they don't really care. Simply throwing money at a problem, as the Canadian government has done, after the report on the findings of the residential schools disaster was published, does not fix anything.

This story covers a period of three years, 2013 to 2016, and serves to expose the failures, incompetence, or simply the maliciousness of the Alberta government's department of Child and

Family Services and their attack on our three-year-old grandson and our family.

Based on our firsthand exposure to this department, while trying to rescue our grandson from foster care, we will clearly document and illustrate to you, for our specific case, the lack of concern for children and their families, the cover-ups, fabrication of information, abuse to both children and families, corruption, and many more diabolical activities for which we or you, or anyone other than Child and Family Services staff, would potentially face prison terms. But due to the systemic corruption in this department the abusers go unpunished. Even more horrific, they are protected by their supervisors, management, and elected officials.

We had the great misfortune to deal with the South Calgary office of Alberta Human Services located in High River, Alberta. However, during our two-year-plus ordeal they in turn referred many decisions to, or sought help from, other South Calgary offices which only provided further proof to us of the systemic corruption and incompetence within the entire department of Child and Family Services Alberta (CFSA).

In case you are asking yourself whether or not we tried the political route, the answer is yes. Our MLA at that time was Danielle Smith. Although we visited her office on many occasions, spoke with her assistant, left copies of correspondence, emailed her, and tried everything to get her involved, she didn't have even enough decency to tell us that she would not help us. She merely led us on, never meeting with us, but with her assistant covering for her by telling us that "Danielle was looking into it." Since she was our MLA we felt so thoroughly betrayed.

We also wrote to the minister of Human Services, Manmeet Bhullar, at that time. However, neither he nor his office had enough decency to even acknowledge any of our letters or emails. When he was replaced by Heather Klimchuk, we thought our chances of getting a hearing with the minister might improve, but she proved even worse. Her approach was to pass our correspondence on to the perpetrators of the abuse, resulting in their retaliation and simply laughing at us. Ask us what our opinion is of elected officials, especially representing the department of Human Services or for that matter our absent, non-caring MLA?

This provides the briefest of overviews of our dealings with Child and Family Services Alberta. In the following chapters we get into the very details of our case. Since the government of Alberta prohibits publication of details that identify children and/or their families in those cases where children are or were in "care of the government," we waited until we had full guardianship and parenting responsibility for our grandson before publishing this book. And because so much harm was caused to our grandson by government of Alberta staff, government of Alberta appointees, and foster parents, we identify all perpetrators in order to protect families that might fall prey to the same system and the same people in the future. It is our intent to completely expose the evildoers that played significant roles in abusing our grandson and causing irreparable damage to our family. Hopefully the evidence provided in the following chapters will generate or at least ignite a sense of accountability within our justice system, so that the perpetrators are investigated, and remedial action is taken. But at the very least, and to prevent this ongoing miscarriage of justice, these perpetrators must have their employment terminated for cause as soon as possible.

In order to provide details as factually as possible for this book, we asked our lawyer for copies of everything in our file.

We also asked him for the return of approximately 700 pages of documentation (340 pages with writing on both sides) that we loaned to him (our property that we obtained from our previous lawyer and Child and Family Services as well as the originals of letters to and from various elected officials) but he refused. We paid all of his fees plus any and all cost of services, but he told us that he worked under a trust condition with the director of Child and Family Services and he must get a release from the director to be able to return to us *our own documents*. Our property is our property and refusing to return same is theft! If our lawyer's comments are true, then the director of Child and Family Services has too much unlimited authority. How can the director take property that belongs to us and then place conditions on returning it to us? Yet the director was able to receive every document that we wrote, that our support consultant wrote, and that our psychologist wrote. That is an affront to any law-abiding person. Who was our lawyer working for and what kind of bogeyman is the director who shows absolutely no regard for people, property, and the law? And in our court proceedings various "director" representatives, ranging from lawyers to caseworkers, were recognized by the court as acting as the director or on behalf of the director. Wow!

Only people who have been through the process of trying to rescue their child or loved one from CFSA arrogance, interference, and confinement can appreciate the monumental task that they face. Although there are some resources such as elected members of the legislature, the Law Society of Alberta, the Ombudsman's office, the Child and Youth Advocacy office, the Office of Freedom of Information and Privacy, and the Human Rights Commission, in our case and mainly because of the publication ban or the perceived invincibility of CFSA, none of these showed any real desire to help, or had any impact when they did. Most disappointing was the Law Society of Alberta which asked for information to support our complaint against our lawyer, and then everything disappeared seemingly into a black hole without a single update, contact, letter, nothing. Obviously monitoring member potential misconduct is not important, rather protecting the member is!

In our attempt to stay within the law and for the purposes of this book we have changed our grandson's name to Gabriel, my son's name to Jackson, and his partner's name to Janet. Since publishing my name or that of my husband would contravene the law, we cannot disclose our identities, but for real and valid reasons or for more in-depth information you may leave messages at our website which we monitor daily.

It is critically important that the reader understands that we experienced horrific treatment at the hands of Child and Family Services Alberta, the foster family, and CFSA agents, and although we make what we believe and know to be factual statements supported by disclosure documents, this book represents OUR OPINION! The opinions expressed by Child and Family Services Alberta and the foster family would differ very significantly from ours.

Should you wish to contact us for more information or to provide any details that you may have of more cases such as ours, please leave details at the following website and someone will definitely contact you on our behalf: corruptcfsa@outlook.com

CHAPTER 1

Historical Background

In order that you, the reader, will understand how or why CFSA (Child and Family Services Alberta) came into or lives, we provide background in the form of some historical and family details.

When most of the involvement with Child and Family Services Alberta started, I was a 68-year-old married woman (second marriage), married to a 74-year-old somewhat disabled man (also second marriage). We were married in 2006 and have a very good marriage; we both have two boys ranging in age from 40 to 46. Unfortunately, my 43-year-old son, Jackson, has suffered from illegal drug abuse for more than 20 years. The other three boys are well-adjusted contributors to society.

Since my second husband and I have been together, we have seen a serious deterioration in my son's judgement regardless of whether or not he is using drugs. One of the strengths of a mother is the inherent ability to instinctively know when a son is "under the influence," and that ability is extremely strong in my particular case. Over a period of five to six years, 2003 to 2009, the relationship between me and my son deteriorated to the point that in 2007 I (we, my husband and I) told him to stay out of our lives. There are so many valid reasons for such a decision, but it was gut-wrenching nonetheless. My son had become so very disrespectful, demanding, and abusive that many times his actions almost became physical threats.

After a period of relative peace, 2007 to late 2009, we received a phone call from my son Jackson asking to talk and requesting our advice. He related that while in drug rehab he met a lady with whom he had sex and she was now pregnant. He said that over the period of 2007 to 2009 he had changed for the better, and he was prepared to assume responsibility for the coming child, but that he needed some help from us. He wanted an opportunity for both him and his partner Janet to learn if they could become a couple and thereby raise the child together.

We found this newfound sense of responsibility quite refreshing and determined to help where we could. Our assistance meant that we met Janet, and we were sometimes impressed with her stories of working as a cook or chef. But when we learned that she had abandoned four children and was divorced from her husband primarily due to her drug and alcohol abuse, we feared that my son's new life was starting on a very tenuous note. However, we were reassured by both my son and his partner that they really wanted to make things work and that he would find a good, high-paying job so that he could support her and a new baby. And she also reassured "everyone" that she had been totally clean at the time the baby was conceived, and she remained clean.

Realizing that they were working very hard at honoring their commitments, we determined to help them find suitable living accommodations. Together we reviewed rental properties, apartments, and condos, but found that rents were extremely expensive. Then we researched condos for sale; and my son found what seemed like good value in a 1,400-square-foot condo in Okotoks. We placed an offer and it was accepted. However, since we committed a sizeable down payment, to protect our investment, we placed three conditions on Jackson and Janet: 1) they must provide a safe, loving home for the baby, 2) no illegal substances on our premises, and 3) no reneging on payments. If all conditions were fully met, we were prepared to eventually gift them the condo.

Baby Gabriel was born in November 2010 and everything seemed to be going well. And for approximately one and a half years everyone seemed happy. My son carried through with finding and working at a high-paying job and Janet prepared good, wholesome meals for their family as a stay-at-home mom. However, as grandparents we held high expectations including cleanliness in the condo and outdoor exercise with the baby.

Slowly the honeymoon was coming to an end. We learned that my son and Janet were not compatible and were involved in open hostilities, many times in front of our grandson who was now just over one and a half years old. Both "parents" were great at escalating any dispute into a very hostile fight. And yes, each blamed the other, so trying to find some positives to build on became almost impossible. Whenever my antennae detected possible confrontations, we quickly removed our grandson Gabriel from the condo and brought him to our home for peace, safety, and love.

The open hostility between the two "parents" slowly caused both to start using drugs again. Now we were keenly watching for any indication of drug use as well as hostilities, but this infuriated both parents. We were told to get out of their lives and that they didn't need any help raising their baby.

Although both parents always blamed the other for starting arguments and for any escalation when they used drugs, we learned that my son had become a "functioning" addict and relied on a binge on drugs every six to eight weeks, whereas Janet had become a habitual user. This was dangerous for our Gabriel and we forced ourselves to interfere more often to ensure his safety. However, my son still wanted to rescue their relationship and often asked us if Janet and Gabriel could live with us while he was working in Northern Alberta for periods of nine or ten days in succession over three-week periods. With us living on acreage, Janet's ability to access drugs was very restricted.

Being more intimately involved in our grandson's life exposed us to so many situations that caused us to rethink whether my son or Janet could ever become caring, loving parents, and we really feared that left on their own they would definitely lose Gabriel to Child and Family Protective Services. Throughout 2012 and the better part of 2013, we became very concerned that Janet had become depressed. She kept the condo in almost total darkness; hardly ever took our grandson out even though there was a children's play park across the small parking lot; had difficulty making friends, etc. Even more disconcerting were the phone calls from my son almost demanding that we "get over right away as this kid is such a pain" or "come and get him because we are using" or the phone call from their attendance at a wedding telling us "this kid is in the way, come and get him." Unfortunately, there are far too many examples, some much more nasty, that it became obvious that our grandson was in an increasingly risky if not, in our opinion, dangerous situation. Ironically, Gabriel, even given the terrible living conditions he was in, was a well-adjusted, happy, compassionate, and very intelligent little boy. Most of our friends instantly took a liking to him. They found him to be eager to help, never cranky, and very loving. So we now have a conundrum. We really believe that our grandson should live with his biological mother and father, but with his life in constant chaos is that fair to him? He is the innocent child and the parents seem to choose drugs over their son. We really love him unconditionally, and know that when he is with us he feels loved and appears to be very happy. He never cries or complains and our friends as well as our visitors are now encouraging us to keep him for longer and longer periods to limit his exposure to "unfit" parents. But we don't have authority to totally remove our grandson from his parents in order to keep him from potential harm.

In August 2013, Janet attended a rehab center in Calgary. While there my son brought Gabriel to see her on two successive Saturdays, but she insisted that he was NOT to bring Gabriel to see her on the third Saturday because she wanted to get her nails done. This, after not seeing her son for many weeks! This filled Jackson with rage and unfortunately he took it out on Gabriel by virtually throwing him through our front door when he returned him to our home. We realized that a very difficult decision was fast approaching.

And this brings us to the event that initially resulted in CFSA involvement.

While Janet was living with us on October 11, 2013, Gabriel awoke very early that morning, 5:45 a.m. As I had not slept that night and was very tired, I took him to his mother's room so that she could care for him while I tried to get some rest. To everyone's surprise the room was empty! Sometime during the night, she had let herself out through the downstairs patio doors, without shoes, made it to the driveway, and into her Jeep. We assume that she was in desperate need of drugs. However, she had a single-car accident, never made it to purchase drugs, and was forced to phone a friend who took her to the Black

Diamond Hospital for medical assistance. It was while she was being treated that she became incoherent and screamed for her son to be brought to her. Black Diamond medical staff, recognizing her symptoms, called CFSA.

In the morning hours of October 11, 2013, I received a phone call from someone named Darcy representing CFSA, asking if my grandson was with me. Darcy then apprised me of the reason for his call, and I advised him that my grandson was with me, safe, well, and happy. Following this episode, Jackson insisted that he and I apply for guardianship of Gabriel as he could no longer trust the care of his son to Janet. We also agreed that while my son was out of town at work, Gabriel would reside with my husband and me, and we would return him to the care of Jackson for only one to three days when my son was back home between work shifts. Also, his sponsor from Narcotics Anonymous had moved into the condo as further "security" and/or encouragement for Jackson to refrain from drug use, and to ensure that when my grandson Gabriel was in the care of my son (only two to three days every two weeks) there was in-house help if required. On October 17, 2013, Jackson and I attended court to obtain custody and guardianship of Gabriel.

This arrangement appeared to be working well. On November 23, my grandson's third birthday, my husband created a special meal for us along with a "special" carrot birthday cake. It was a great birthday! Now Janet was spending much more time at our home and showed no interest in taking any craft courses or doing anything outdoors with Gabriel (or indoors for that matter). Although she and Jackson still fought constantly, they both insisted that they wanted to be a family. Some improvement actually took place, but it was short lived. Although my grandson really treasured the time with his father, we had to be diligent to ensure that the bull-in-the-china-shop approach of my son didn't result in abuse to our grandson. When they went swimming, for instance, Jackson's swimming ability gave Gabriel so much confidence in the water. My grandson even told everyone how much fun he had with his dad.

We celebrated my younger son Anthony's birthday December 20 at his favorite restaurant, Smugglers. That night Jackson insisted that he and Anthony should do some bonding, even though we insisted that the idea was very flawed. But there was no reasoning with Jackson. So, we brought our grandson home with us and waited to hear from his dad … one night … one day and night … one more day and night. Then came December 23, court day for the guardianship hearing. Both my son and I were to appear in court, but late December 22 we heard from Jackson saying that he could not attend and he demanded that I also not attend. From his voice I came to realize that he had been using drugs and advised him that I would honor my commitment to attend, which immediately caused a verbal eruption of blasphemies.

When our case was called, it became somewhat obvious to me that there was another interested party in attendance. The judge asked where my son was and I advised him that my son phoned me to tell me that he was unable to attend. The judge pursued the reason and I said that I thought he had used drugs two or three days earlier, so he did not want to come to court. A lady also addressed the judge and she suggested or recommended to the judge that I be granted interim guardianship and further recommended that I be granted by court order "parentship" of my grandson as well. The judge agreed and told me to wait until after the noon adjournment to pick up the completed and signed court orders. I then learned that this lady was a representative from Child and Family Services Alberta.

This was a mixed blessing. On one hand, I now had authority and responsibility granted by the court to look after my grandson. On the other hand, my attendance at court had aroused such anger in Jackson that every attempt at conversation was turned into an outright war. And this carried on into Christmas Day as my son continued to be "messed-up" by drugs; he was verbally abusive and physically violent to me, to my husband, to Gabriel, and to Janet. Everyone paid for his use of drugs; no one escaped.

Finally, his condition improved by December 31, to the point that he felt comfortable enough under our supervision to take Gabriel to the Okotoks Recreation Centre to use the gym and also to go skating. It was a very good day! But inevitably and as in the past, the good time ended abruptly on January 2, 2014 around 11:00 a.m. when my son's sponsor phoned us to advise that Jackson had gone out on January 1 and had not returned home yet. The sponsor had to leave for work, therefore we needed to collect our grandson as soon as possible. So from this point onward we exercised our parenting responsibility and kept our grandson at our home. Any visitations by my son with Gabriel were now done at our home under our supervision, even though the parenting order gave us the discretion to place our grandson with his dad if everything was going well and the likelihood of trouble seemed very remote.

We registered our grandson at the Montessori preschool and he started on January 7, 2014. He just loved the Montessori program, but the interaction with other children of his age was paramount. However, the greatest blessing was Sharlene Brown, our grandson's teacher and school administrator. She was completely attuned to our Gabriel's plight and really focused on character issues, building relationships with other children, and helping him understand how things work. Although he attended preschool from noon till 2:30 p.m. every Tuesday and Wednesday, he begged for more exposure to school. On the off-days he often asked if he could go to school to see his friends.

With Jackson's sponsor living at the condo, we noticed a marked improvement in the relationship between my son and Janet. They attended AA (Alcoholics Anonymous) and NA (Narcotics Anonymous) meetings two to three times weekly, ate wholesome meals, took greater interest in keeping the condo neat and clean, and Jackson even asked me to accompany him to see a psychologist recommended in his rehab program. Given that Gabriel really wanted to see his dad and the continuing improvement within Jackson's household, we chanced returning Gabriel to his condo for one or two days weekly. But Jackson never relented with regard to his disapproval of my guardianship and parentship of Gabriel. He voiced very strong feelings on April 16, 2014 at court when the judge extended the guardianship and parentship orders for an additional three months. CFSA was now much involved in our case mainly because of Jackson's insistence that he and Janet resume responsibility for and custody of their child. CFSA seriously considered returning Gabriel to Jackson and Janet providing that they would commit to and fulfill several conditions for a minimum period of three months: 1) complete abstinence from all addictive substances, 2) no violence, swearing, or fighting in the presence of Gabriel, and 3) continuing to work diligently at Jackson's job in order to meet all obligations. And we were prepared to support CFSA as we continued to believe that it was possible, or even probable for these parents to pull their act together for the sake of their son.

Then came May 1–10, 2014, when a friend of Jackson's invited Jackson to come to Leduc to help him with several projects for which he was willing to pay. Since Jackson was waiting for a job reassignment, he decided that this would be an ideal opportunity to reintroduce himself to "old friends" while making some money. Janet vehemently opposed Jackson's plan as did we and his father, Trevor. Since we all knew that Jackson's drug use started in Leduc many years ago with these same friends, we did all we could to stop Jackson from going, but in vain.

During the 11 days Jackson was in Leduc, he ran into trouble with the law and spent over $1,100 on what we believe was drugs. He did not bring home a single penny. But more importantly, Jackson's BIG opportunity that was granted to him by CFSA was completely dead after only two and a half weeks. His so-called love of his son didn't even last three weeks let alone the three months provided by CFSA. Now CFSA dictated that Gabriel was to remain with us, in our home, without access to his mother or father. The violence between Jackson and Janet resumed until Janet finally decided to leave Jackson for her own protection and safety. Since Gabriel and Janet had never bonded, the impact on Gabriel was minimal. But the "bully" had to have his way. Jackson never took responsibility for his actions; everything that happened was either Janet's fault or my fault. He refused to abide by CFSA-imposed conditions and insisted that they could not touch him or his son, that the court process was a farce, and that we were all conspiring against him. Unfortunately, he never abandoned his holier-than-thou attitude, and his abuse and accompanying violence increased. And for some inexplicable reason, Janet returned to the condo to be with Jackson.

Jackson, Janet, my husband, and I, with Gabriel, met with CFSA caseworker Bonita Hoffman-Russell on May 22, 2014 in

High River to review her prepared documents where she summarized threats, undertakings, work already accomplished, and work still to be done. Then Bonita clearly advised everyone that CFSA would normally have apprehended Gabriel by this time, but she was giving Jackson and Janet three more months to prove that they could be "fit" parents. She emphasized that this was their final chance and her last concession.

We received a call from Jackson on May 28, 2014 advising us that he had "kicked out" Janet and she had taken her Jeep with her, leaving him without a vehicle for work. He wanted to borrow my husband's Suburban. My husband did not want to give Jackson access to his truck but when Jackson insisted that he would only use it to drive to and from work and since Janet was now gone, she would not have access, my husband relented. We are constantly wrestling with whether we are acting responsibly or actually enabling Jackson's drug use. So, since Jackson had to leave for work and did not have transportation from the condo to come for the Suburban, I drove to the condo to pick him up and bring him to our home. En route, as I was driving, I mentioned to him that his stupidity put him in very real danger of completely losing Gabriel. Instead of apologizing and admitting that he needed to work harder at improving, he became violent and grabbed my neck as if trying to choke me. I instinctively swung my arm and hit him in the face, causing him to let go of my neck. I did not tell my husband immediately, but waited till Jackson had left our house with the Suburban. He became so angry that he threatened to go after him; but after some consideration decided to phone CFSA and the caseworker now handling our case, Bonita Hoffman-Russell. Bonita said that she would phone Jackson to help diffuse the situation. Less than one hour later, just after 5 p.m., she phoned us to tell us that we were in grave danger, that we should immediately pack a bag for Gabriel, and go to the Okotoks RCMP detachment and wait for her, which we did. We were very conflicted as Bonita never told us what she learned from her phone call with Jackson. Although Jackson has often been a bully, he has always backed down when challenged. While we waited for Bonita to arrive at the RCMP detachment we reviewed everything that happened and also considered Jackson's 40 years of history, but never did we encounter any life-threatening violence. What could Bonita have uncovered? And wasn't she supposed to diffuse the situation not aggravate it?

CHAPTER 2

CFSA Deception

When Bonita arrived at RCMP Okotoks detachment office the evening of May 28, 2014, she again told us that our lives were in grave danger. However, she refused to tell us what she learned from Jackson so we were dubious about any of her claims, especially when she asked us to wait in the holding room so that she could speak privately to the RCMP officer. But she kept reiterating that the lives of all three of us were in grave danger.

Bonita was busily making phone calls to various people and then asked if we might go somewhere for supper as the paperwork would take some time to finalize. At supper Bonita told us that she did not want us to return to our home because of this "mortal danger," and that Gabriel needed to go somewhere safe; where his father could not find him. After brain storming for an hour or so we suggested that Gabriel might be safe at a distant relative's house in Okotoks. Bonita asked that we immediately contact this individual to ask if they would shelter Gabriel until the danger passed. That individual, (let's call her Mrs. Foster), said that she definitely would take Gabriel for the danger period and we drove there to deliver our grandson. Although this distant relative's family was not known to Gabriel, we felt that since she had children all at or close to Gabriel's age, he might appreciate their company. We hoped this would minimize the trauma of the upcoming period of time.

We returned to RCMP Okotoks detachment around 9:45 p.m. with Bonita and we were then pressured by two RCMP officers and Bonita to file an Emergency Protection Order (EPO) against Jackson restricting him from any access to me, my husband, Gabriel, and any area within 250 meters of our home. Although we were certain that this measure was a complete overreaction to the situation, we learned that without the protection order we could lose custody of Gabriel. Since we had been at RCMP Okotoks detachment from 5:30 p.m. and it was now approaching 11:40 p.m., the pressure to have us sign the order became overbearing and I finally signed. After signing the order Bonita and the RCMP insisted that we not return home but rather use our motor home to take a short vacation until the extreme danger subsided. Instead, we returned home, slept for the night, and the next morning moved the motor home to a friend's property and went to Banff for three days. But the stress of all the proceedings of May 28 took its toll as my husband contracted shingles while in Banff. And till this day he has not recovered from the nerve damage to his upper right side, right hand, and fingers.

When we returned home we closely examined our property, home, garage, and garden shed to determine if anything had been disturbed or damaged, but found nobody had been on our property. We then went to Mrs. Foster's house to collect Gabriel. With an EPO there was little chance that danger would come anywhere near our home. Besides, with a quarter-mile-long dirt and gravel driveway we could easily see and hear anyone or any vehicle approaching us.

Gabriel told us that he enjoyed the time at Mrs. Foster's, especially his time playing with the "kids." With this knowledge Mrs. Foster suggested that they, whenever practical and convenient, have Gabriel sleep over or even have Gabriel accompany them on a vacation or two; but that I would have final say and I would approve all arrangements. I was favorably impressed and saw this arrangement as a way of sharing the work and responsibility of caring for Gabriel with what appeared to be a well-intentioned family, and Gabriel would have playmates. I told her that we would reimburse her family for any and all expenses incurred on Gabriel's behalf.

Over the period of June through August 2014, the Foster family occasionally had Gabriel sleep over, took him on short camping trips, etc. And Gabriel seemed quite happy. So, with Gabriel relatively happy, although he still asked for his father, access to the Fosters' children appeared to bridge the gap. Gabriel continued to live with us and spend more time with the Fosters. We even "babysat" Gabriel and the Foster children at their house on two separate occasions. Yes, even though Jackson and Janet separately continued their destructive ways, Gabriel saw less and less of them and concentrated on the final days of his Montessori preschool, his friends, and alternating between us and the Fosters. Occasionally, Gabriel still asked to see his dad. And being ever so positive about the future we tried to fit in some CFSA supervised visits between "parents" and Gabriel.

June 3, 2014 required another court hearing to review my Guardianship Order. But since I now had an EPO I needed to advise the court security that Jackson and I were to not have any contact. They promised that they would carefully watch for any potential trouble. That morning when Jackson, accompanied by Janet, entered the 12th floor of the courthouse, he saw me and angrily headed directly for me. Both Mr. and Mrs. Foster intercepted him until court security took over. But the worst possible thing happened next; both Jackson and Janet told the court that they did not want me to have custody or guardianship of Gabriel, and they would prefer/demand that he be placed in foster care. Also, they asked that no family member should have custody or guardianship of Gabriel! The blood drained from me and I could feel myself fainting; which I did on the court steps. Luckily the court sheriff caught me and stopped my fall. EMS was called and I learned that I had suffered a mini-stroke.

Notwithstanding my medical situation, I was plagued by Jackson's and Janet's comments or "orders" in court. How could so-called parents of an innocent, love-starved, and very com-passionate child forbid family members from caring for him and stress that he be placed in foster care? Should they ever be allowed to have any access to Gabriel? Such statements usually come back to bite you; will these? And I wrestled with a horrible feeling; after working so hard to keep my son from completely losing Gabriel to CFSA and foster care, Jackson now blames me for everything and he HATES me. Yes, I admonished him but it was for his own good…and it didn't have any effect other than to increase whatever contempt he has for me.

After EMS gave me the "tentative OK" to leave, the Fosters insisted that we immediately visit RCMP Okotoks to apprise them of Jackson's actions in the courthouse, which we reluc-tantly did. RCMP asked each of us to complete paperwork to clearly describe what happened. They then advised that the EPO needed to be extended and increased from 250 meters to 500 meters, and that Jackson should no longer be allowed in Okotoks as the Fosters and Gabriel's preschool were both in Okotoks and easily accessible. RCMP also recommended that anyone that shared in the caring for Gabriel needed to become extra vigilant which included not only us, but also the Foster family and Gabriel's Montessori preschool. They also recommended that we make our neighbors aware of potential dangers, and for them to make note of strange or unknown people or unknown vehicles. Unfortunately, these events took away Jackson's living accommodations and he needed to find alternate housing arrangements outside of Okotoks. Since our finances could not support carrying the condo payments and cost of utilities for any more than three months, we busied ourselves with fixing walls, repainting, etc., in order to list the condo for sale. The hope of granting eventual ownership to Jackson had now evaporated, mainly due to him contravening all three conditions that we had imposed on him. Yes, it seemed absolutely cruel of the RCMP to remove Jackson from Okotoks, but RCMP experience clearly showed that the condo was in very real danger of becoming a crack house if we had not acted swiftly. Although Jackson did not have any ownership interest in the condo, other than paying monthly rent and his utilities, he became hostile and demanded that any capital gain be given to him. Imagine, he brought illicit drugs into the condo; exposed his baby to those drugs and drug dealers; missed several rent payments, in one case, resulting in a fraud charge by our bank; had a heated dispute with the gas company which we had to settle, and his antics resulted in two banks cancelling our joint account; and he demands the proceeds of any capital gain? For what, more drugs?

We quickly learned that Jackson and Janet committed irreparable damage at court, not only to themselves but to us as well. Now CFSA and others indicated that even the judge could not avoid some reluctance at continuing my guardianship. Also, support staff and several lawyers told us that with dissension running rampant in the family it would be difficult to justify an order whereby Gabriel should continue to reside with us. However Jackson seemed intent on destroying all chances the family could have of being granted custody of Gabriel. He showed absolutely no concern for his own son. Janet was a nonentity as she followed Jackson's lead, but Gabriel still never asked about her or for her.

The Fosters, seeing the turmoil caused by Jackson, offered to keep Gabriel for longer and longer periods, and their children started to ask if they could "keep" Gabriel. We did some activities as an extended family with the Fosters, sharing experiences of their children as well as experiences of Gabriel.

Bonita Hoffman-Russell, the CFSA caseworker, took a more than passing interest in how effectively we worked with the Fosters. She often said that we had picked wisely and found an ideal family if Gabriel was to be adopted. Notwithstanding Jackson's animosity and demonstrated hatred towards me and my husband, we always held out hope that he would find appropriate treatment, be able to fully recover, and get his son back. When Bonita again approached the possibility of potential adoption by the Fosters we were quick to place a caveat that the Fosters would have to agree to Jackson having access to Gabriel if and when Jackson could prove he took all required treatment programs, passed them successfully, and was fully recovered. Life continued for Gabriel and us on an even keel.

As Gabriel spent more time with the Fosters, and they clearly showed every intent of potentially becoming guardians and possibly even adoptive parents, we arranged for them to collect most of Gabriel's furniture, clothing, and toys and move them to their house, hopefully giving Gabriel even more familiarity as he transitioned. This served a dual purpose; 1) to help us clear the condo to prepare it for showing, and 2) to keep heirloom toys (collected and given to my boys) together so they could be eventually returned to my boys. We had accumulated special Fisher Price toys and other quality pieces for Jackson and Anthony as they were growing up, and both boys had gladly presented most of these to Gabriel with the understanding that their specific toys would be returned to them after Gabriel was finished with them. We helped Mr. Foster move Gabriel's convertible bed for which we felt that we had paid a fortune, and all of Gabriel's Fisher Price toys that he simply treasured such as his safari set, camper, airplane, and too many others to itemize. And Gabriel would tell us how he enjoyed having his own toys. Everything seemed to be going so well.

Mr. Foster came to our home on August 7 to pick up his travel trailer, and while having coffee on our deck said that he was so extremely pleased that Gabriel had fit in so well with his children, and that everyone was looking forward to tomorrow's planned vacation with Gabriel. Mrs. Foster would be packing the trailer the next day but we should pick up Gabriel at 1:00 p.m. and keep him till 4:00 p.m. so that we could get a last-minute visit with Gabriel before the two to three-day holiday, but also to give Mrs. Foster some alone time to get things ready. Gabriel was really looking forward to getting away and camping.

The next day, August 8, 2014, is a day I will never forget. We were busy working on the condo as it was almost ready to list, when at 1:00 p.m. we stopped to phone Mr. Foster to see if we could drive over to pick up Gabriel. When Mr. Foster told us that things were bad and we could not collect Gabriel, we feared that something was terribly wrong. Since Mr. Foster had visited his doctor that morning, we feared that perhaps he received some bad news, so we waited till 3.35 p.m. and without any word from Mr. Foster, decided to go to the Foster residence. Mr. Foster was home but his reaction to our visit showed that he really didn't want us there and he hesitated when we asked if we could go in. Once inside, he told us he was home alone with Gabriel but things were very bad. We needed some disclosure from him so I said that I would go to the backyard to visit with Gabriel while Mr. Foster talked to my husband. Then Mr. Foster divulged a horrible story.

Bonita Hoffman-Russell had phoned Mrs. Foster the previous evening (the evening that Mr. Foster was at our house telling us how good everything was with Gabriel) to tell her she was closing the file. Why not phone us, we are the guardians, we don't know. Mrs. Foster asked Bonita if she would receive funding for looking after Gabriel, to which Bonita replied, "No." The only way that the Fosters would receive payment was if CFSA apprehended Gabriel. But as Jackson was gainfully employed and earning significant money, Mrs. Foster should phone Jackson to see if he would offset some of her costs. Remember that we offered to fully reimburse the Fosters for all expenses incurred on behalf of Gabriel. Anyway, Jackson's father, Trevor, answered the phone since Jackson was away camping, and when Mrs. Foster asked him about Jackson helping out financially, Mrs. Foster said Trevor's response was "do you have a death wish?" Mrs. Foster then immediately phoned Bonita advising that her life and the lives of all her family were in danger, as well as Gabriel's life. Bonita immediately told Mrs. Foster that they would arrange to apprehend Gabriel using the excuse that he was in mortal danger. That way the Fosters would receive financial assistance. Although I was Gabriel's court-appointed guardian with responsibility for parenting Gabriel, Bonita and

Mrs. Foster conspired behind my back to "kidnap" my grandson from me. Is this how the so-called protectors of children are supposed to act; removing children from family to place them into a potentially dangerous situation and into foster care? However, there was no threat; only Mrs. Foster's version of a stupid statement from someone not thinking clearly, which Trevor strongly denies having said anyway. Mr. Foster then told my husband that we were not to know, but Bonita and her assistant were on their way to finalize arrangements. Remember that my husband and I, along with Gabriel and our property, were all protected by an EPO. Therefore, we were never in danger nor was Gabriel while in our custody. Even the Child, Youth and Family Enhancement (CYFE) Act and Agreements and Orders clearly state that no apprehension should take place when a less intrusive measure is available. More worrisome to us was the fact that had we not gone to the Foster house unannounced, Gabriel would have been taken away by CFSA without our knowledge even though we are his family and have guardianship.

Mrs. Foster returned home just minutes before Bonita and her assistant arrived and made it very clear that she was not happy that my husband and I were there. We seemed to have disrupted CFSA's and Mrs. Foster's devious plans. Bonita made it clear to us that she had prepared all the paperwork and there was no backtracking. We strenuously argued that Jackson would never deliberately injure any family member and that our EPO protected Gabriel as well as us, so we were taking Gabriel home with us. Bonita became very indignant, and with the help of Mr. and Mrs. Foster, asserted that we could not protect Gabriel and he was their primary concern. The EPO was completely discounted as worthless. Then Bonita "promised" that she had planned a two-stage process whereby we could see Gabriel as long as no one divulges where Gabriel was located. No matter how strongly we argued, Bonita discounted every argument and said she now had final approval from the judge, so they were taking Gabriel to the High River office to put everything in process. I really wanted my husband to just take Gabriel away from them and go home, but we were told that we were breaking the law. What law justifies abusing a three-and-a-half-year-old child? Then Bonita told Gabriel that she and Mrs. Foster were taking him to a meeting in High River. I will never forget my beautiful three-and-a-half-year-old grandson coming to us to proudly tell us he was en route to a meeting in High River. My husband and I still cry every time we remember that horrible deception to our beautiful grandson. What I will also never forget is Mrs. Foster packing Gabriel's things without any concerns, without tears, without emotions, nothing! Now I realized the type of person I had trusted. She was going to get her financing, not just the reimbursements we had promised, and that's all that mattered. And she and Bonita had planned the whole scenario. As Gabriel was being rushed away, Mr. Foster had tears as well but weeks later under different circumstances we had real reason to question if he had simply been acting.

Two hours later Mrs. Foster returned to the Foster house and very coolly announced that she went with Bonita to the "foster home" and Gabriel seemed happy as there were other kids there. The foster home was new and looked really good, and she would have daily access to Gabriel. I am the guardian and blood relative, but Bonita has taken away all my court-appointed rights and given them to Mrs. Foster. What was going on? I told Mrs. Foster exactly what I thought of her, of her deceitful actions, and of the collusion between her and Bonita. I also questioned that since the Fosters were supposedly threatened and, unlike us, they had not taken the necessary safety-proofing precautions, why did Gabriel go to them? The Fosters could easily be followed to the foster home, as we did without their knowledge on August 12, 2014. But CFSA gave them total control of our grandson, even against their own policies, something that will be addressed in later chapters.

Three days later Bonita arranged with Mrs. Foster, mainly because of our constant pressure to see Gabriel, to have a family dinner at a South Calgary restaurant so that we could see how well Gabriel was doing. My younger son Anthony also attended, and I have only seen him cry once, on the death of my mother, but he actually broke down and cried when he saw what CFSA and Mrs. Foster had done to his little nephew. This beautiful, loving little boy actually hit one of the Foster girls because of his fear, loneliness, and trauma, as well as both physical and mental abuse at the hands of CFSA, the foster home, and Mrs. Foster. After dinner we gathered outside to say our goodbyes, and Gabriel, who was always happy, running, and playing, just laid face down on the lawn with tears streaming down his face. It was too much for me and my husband to bear. We determined to do everything in our power to fight these inhuman, lying, abusive child and family destroyers.

The next day, at Bonita's request, Bonita met us at the Fosters' house where we overheard her explain the paperwork to Mrs. Foster for all the promised financial assistance. After Mrs. Foster signed the paperwork, my husband and I looked at each other and we both had the story of Judas and the 30 pieces of silver foremost in our minds. Bonita warned us that any challenge to CFSA would result in us going broke because CFSA had a slate of lawyers that would keep us in court until we were bankrupt. Nevertheless, we had to rescue our grandson, and so we started what seemed like the impossible task of finding a lawyer to represent us. Most lawyers told us that nobody can win against CFSA. The Child Youth and Family Enhancement Act (CYFEA) bestows so much power on the director of Child and Family Services that CFSA can defeat virtually any challenge. They can use hearsay without investigating (which they did) and present that information in court as fact (which they did), something no one else would ever be allowed to do.

Having developed a relationship with the Okotoks detachment of the RCMP, we visited them and provided them with a summary of Gabriel's apprehension and Bonita's threats to us. The corporal said that CFSA acted illegally; they broke the law. With this newfound information we called Bonita's supervisor, Shauna Asselstine, to share our findings with her and to ask for a meeting with her. She vociferously told us that "their law doesn't apply to us" and she hung up. Talk about arrogance and ignorance! And of course there was NO meeting.

Bonita advised us that a court hearing was set for August 18, 2014, and that we should attend. Just prior to court coming to session, Bonita moved into the seat beside me and asked me to sign some documents. Being very leery, I said that I would read them before I signed anything. And that's when all my fears were reconfirmed. Bonita was applying for a Permanent Guardianship Order (PGO) asking the court to permanently remove Gabriel from my guardianship and give permanent guardianship of my grandson to the director of Child and Family Services to do whatever that position dictated. As I read further, I found almost the entire document was fraught with fabrications, lies, misrepresentations, etc., anything to support her application for PGO.

In Bonita's affidavit at the beginning of the PGO application she says, "The child needs intervention. To protect the child's survival, security or development, the child cannot live with the guardian because…The guardian could no longer provide long-term care for Gabriel and that she would be returning him to his parents." This is completely untrue; total fiction and a fabrication to support her application!

On page two in the first paragraph Bonita writes: "Shortly after this occurred (the guardian) arranged for Gabriel to live with extended family as she felt she could no longer care for Gabriel and keep him safe." This is nothing but lies! It was Bonita that wanted us to let Gabriel stay with the "extended non-family."

Further on page two Bonita writes, "continued to use drugs and to engage in fighting and yelling with Jackson hitting and punching Janet including when their child Gabriel was present. Jackson was also aggressive with his mother often intimidating her and demanding she let him take Gabriel even when (the guardian) was concerned Gabriel would not be safe." Note, none of this is factual or true. It is written simply to support her case for PGO. Jackson was always a bully and potential problem and we were prepared for his out-of-sorts behavior to continue; but Bonita wanted to use Jackson's behavioral problems against us in support of her chosen "extended family."

On bottom of page three Bonita further states, "On 2014/04/17 a further report was received with concerns that (the guardian) could no longer provide long-term care for Gabriel and that she would be returning him to his parents." Again, more lies to support her application. Where is the report she refers to? I'll bet it doesn't exist.

In the third paragraph of page two Bonita writes, "Jackson was reportedly making threats against those caring for Gabriel and concerns Jackson was stalking the caregivers." The threats, if any, were against the Fosters but Bonita had to lie and use the term "caregivers" to include us and to protect the family she chose to "inherit" Gabriel.

Bonita further writes, "Regarding the guardian, she has reported she cannot provide long-term care to Gabriel and is assisting Children's Services in finding alternative kinship placement." How can this be true? I was fighting with every ounce of energy to have my grandson returned to me! So, needless to say, I refused to sign the PGO application. But it appears that Bonita presented it anyway.

On the last page of the PGO application Bonita writes, "On 2014/05/28 Jackson assaulted (the guardian) while she was driving her car. Jackson choked (the guardian) while Gabriel was in the back seat." Another lie, Gabriel was at home with my husband. All of these lies and fabrications told me that Bonita had already decided that Gabriel was to be permanently removed from my care and given to the babysitters who were really not family. After pointing out all the incorrect information, Bonita asked me once again to sign the document saying that she would make the necessary corrections. With Bonita's history of dishonesty and game playing against us there was no trust, so I once again refused to sign the document. Now it was time to turn the battle into an all-out war.

As the original PGO document was never returned to me by my lawyer, nor can I determine whether or not it was ever filed, I cannot include it in the appendices. In lieu of that document I have included a file copy of Melani Carefoot's questions to our first lawyer for answers regarding all the false statements made by Bonita.

Although we eventually found a lawyer, my husband and I had real concerns about her very soft approach, her strategy, and her willingness to compromise with CFSA. We found out later that most lawyers tried to "negotiate" or compromise because the law or the CYFEA was so supportive of CFSA any conflict with CFSA would quickly be used against any client. That client would face a wall of fabricated information, lies, and hearsay evidence, none supported but used in court as gospel. At this time we knew that in our case, CFSA broke all the rules, created fictional information or scenarios to further their own aims, broke the law, conspired with "babysitters" against a guardian who was also family, and the list goes on. Our lawyer was able to access documents we had never heard of, such as affidavits written by Bonita Hoffman-Russell which, stated as fact that I had said I could not care for Gabriel in the longer term. This was absolutely false. Although I am the court-appointed guardian, my husband and I co-parent. He cooks, occasionally bathes Gabriel, reads bedtime stories, takes him for walks, and helps or "watches" Gabriel play outdoors with his playground equipment. But nobody asked my husband or me; they just chose to fabricate "evidence." Later our lawyer was able to locate the names of those making the false claims, and where in court the comments were supposedly made and was able to prove through court documents that those words never came out of my mouth. But because we felt a necessity to hammer CFSA with their lies in court and our lawyer chose to not rock the boat, we mutually decided to part company. However, she gave us probably the best advice we could have received. She strongly recommended that we use a support resource, Melani Carefoot of Positive Choices Counselling, to help us through all discussions and meetings with CFSA.

Melani had worked for CFSA but became so conflicted with some of their practices that she left their employment to start up her own business helping clients navigate through the pitfalls of dealing with CFSA. Our lawyer identified that we needed Melani's help even more than we needed legal representation.

When we initially met with Melani to review our case, she could not believe the corruption and dirty tricks that CFSA had used against us. Her immediate reaction was for us to find a "good" lawyer with a history of "wins" against CFSA; but that is easier said than done. She also could not believe the response from Shauna Asselstine and undertook to involve the department manager, Don Wijesooria. That is when we fully understood how desperate our case was. During my husband's call to Don Wijesooria, Don actually said, "I will meet with you but if I hear even the remotest hint of anxiety in your voice, I will cancel the meeting, do you understand?" Can you believe such arrogance and ignorance from someone at this level of authority? So, my husband told Don that since we were having great difficulty trying to talk with or meet with anyone at CFSA, we would hire Melani Carefoot as support for us when communicating with CFSA. He immediately told my husband that he would not allow it. When we related Don's comments to Melani she helped us file a request for administrative review against his decision. And here is where Melani's expertise became invaluable. We would never have known about administrative reviews. But in this case, Don Wijesooria immediately phoned us to say that he would fight the administrative review based on the fact that hiring Melani would contravene a section of the CYFEA. However, we persisted with the filing and when he saw the actual paperwork he phoned to tell us to cancel the request for administrative review as he had changed his mind. We could hire Melani but she could not attend our meetings. Since this would have been a useless exercise, we continued with the request for administrative review, which forced Don W to relent and accept

LET'S DESTROY ALBERTA'S FAMILIES

Melani. A series of emails describing the circus orchestrated by Don W is enclosed in the appendices. But his word had no value; he tried ever so desperately to block any of our or Melani's attempts at communicating with caseworkers at CFSA.

Unfortunately, we now realized that we were facing a double whammy: corruption at all levels within CFSA and mercenary babysitters using every dirty trick they knew. As it was now 11 or 12 days since Gabriel's apprehension and because we continued to phone and email Bonita for any information we could get on Gabriel, she finally told us that Gabriel had been returned to the Fosters on or around August 19, 2014. By our calculation Gabriel had been in foster care from August 8, 2014 to August 19, 2014, a total of 11 or 12 days. But we are the guardians with a strong EPO on me, my husband and Gabriel and our property, and CFSA returned our grandson to the unprotected Fosters. Why? Upon receiving this information, my husband sent the following email to the Fosters:

> Mr./ Mrs.—
>
> Bonita told us on Monday that Gabriel would be returned to you yesterday or today at latest. Did she do that? How is Gabriel?

Reply from Mrs. Foster:

> Hi Mr. —
>
> Gabriel is great. Happy, healthy and spending lots of time with us and the kids. How is Mrs. — doing? We have been very concerned about her and hoping she is in a better frame of mind. We are working really

hard to cooperate with Child Protective Services and they have a great plan for Gabriel's future. I don't think we are authorized to talk to anyone about where Gabriel sleeps at night. It would be best if you talked to Bonita about that. We hope life starts improving for you and Mrs. — This has been a rocky road. Things should be much more settled for you both now.

Mrs. Foster

Please remember that the Fosters *conspired* with CFSA to kidnap our grandson but they have no moral compass, no conscience, no shame, and no remorse for what they did or how they did it. Imagine having the gall to say that she hoped I was in a better frame of mind, when she kidnapped my grandson. According to most people that have heard this story they wonder why I didn't just slug her. Mrs. Foster's response set off alarms that told us we were not dealing with a normal person. Mrs. Foster betrayed us, but even more so she betrayed Gabriel, and doesn't have the capability to see or understand what damage she wrought. During our discussions with the myriad of psychologists and counsellors that we were seeing, my husband reiterated this story and several ventured to say that they could see many of the signs of sociopathic behavior, so we needed to be extra careful. If not dealing with a sociopath then we were likely dealing with a narcissist, so in any event we were to never trust anything that came out of her mouth. Also, when visiting with a business acquaintance in Okotoks my husband learned that this person knew Mrs. Foster and told my husband not to trust her in the least. Not really familiar with those terms we quickly went online for definitions which caused both of us to feel quite ill.

My husband and I continued to demand that Bonita honor her promise that we could see Gabriel any time we wanted; all we had to do was ask. But she blocked us from any access for almost three weeks. Finally, Bonita relented and asked that we meet her somewhere in Okotoks. My husband said enough is enough; the visit will be at our home as "I am disabled and can more easily move around my own home." What we did not know was that Bonita insisted that our visits with Gabriel would have to be supervised. What kind of insensitive monster are we dealing with? We raised Gabriel from birth and Bonita wrote accolades in affidavits about Gabriel's upbringing, our excellent parenting, his great personality, his compassion, etc., and now she tells us we need to be supervised when we are with Gabriel. This person really hates us for challenging her and she seems determined to hurt us as much as she can.

All of this trauma took a real toll on my husband and me. We both blamed ourselves and sometimes each other for what Gabriel had to endure. We secretly felt that one of us should have used force to prevent Gabriel's apprehension, although Bonita warned us that we would have been charged with breaking the law. But self-doubt was really testing our resolve and at times our marriage. So, it was with my husband's best intentions that he emailed Mr. and Mrs. Foster to tell them that I was contemplating harming myself, hoping that could be enough motivation for Mrs. Foster to phone me to ask how I was doing, and perhaps rebuild some type of relationship. But he completely misjudged Mrs. Foster. Instead of checking on me she used the email to her advantage to phone the RCMP. That stupid miscalculation by my husband cost me a night at the new Calgary Health Campus under psychological assessment. The positive that came from that experience was the doctor's report that took direct aim at Mrs. Foster for reporting falsely and gave me a clean bill of health. He directly stated that with the horrific stress I was enduring he was surprised that I had not suffered a stroke or heart attack. He also said very clearly that those who sent me to the hospital were in more need of psychological help than I would likely ever need. However, I did tell him that my blood pressure had hit very dangerous highs, to which he replied that was the case when I entered the hospital.

After the unrelenting pressure from me and my husband, Bonita along with a new caseworker, Jessica Smith arranged for a 40-minute visit at our home on or about August 22, 2014. Gabriel had always enjoyed playing on the children's play set that my husband bought and erected. Gabriel would spend so much time with either me or my husband pushing him on his swing, often until my husband could no longer walk and had to crawl to our deck to sit down. But today Gabriel just sat on his swing, his little heart breaking with tears coming down his face.

In an attempt to minimize the damage that Bonita had caused, she started some small talk and caught our attention with this comment: "the Fosters have started to safety proof their house much as you have already done." Our alarm went off again. She fully knew that she removed Gabriel from our safe home and placed him in the Fosters' unprotected house, yet she used Gabriel's safety as her reason for so doing. Is there any limit to how far her lies, fabrications, and deceptions go? Then we learned that Bonita had been taken off our case and was replaced by Jessica Smith. Was that the CFSA way of protecting one of their own by removing her and keeping her out of our sight so that she could escape potential prosecution for breaking the law and harming our grandson?

Then we received this unsolicited email from Mrs. Foster on August 25, 2014:

Hi Mr. & Mrs.—

Just thought I would send an update on how Gabriel is doing. He is great. He had a blast camping this weekend and was happy to have day home back in full swing today. He just loves to play and be with the kids. Here are some pictures from our recent adventures.

Also I truly do hope things are getting better for you, Mrs. — We are truly in a great place with Gabriel and are grateful for our time with him and our other kids, getting settled back into life and are only forward looking. We have so many wonderful resources at our finger tips to help Gabriel and we are receiving so much support to help him heal and move forward. I can't wait to get some of those things up and running. I have received a couple visits in my home by a worker who has given me so much knowledge and tools to help Gabriel the best we can. We are confident and prepared to truly make a difference in his life. I know you worry about the effect his break from us had on him…I can assure you, he is no different now than when he left. He was with us most of the time anyhow…He is a little boy who needs a lot of help to work through and recover from his past, but we knew that before…He is on the right track, smart beyond his years and I know he knows it!

Mrs. Foster

But on the same day Mrs. Foster phoned Jessica Smith (Bonita's replacement at CFSA) and through our review of disclosure documents found this transcription:

August 25, 2014 – Mrs. Foster

- *Overall today Gabriel was not happy and most of his interactions with other children were mean and aggressive. Gabriel was disciplined with timeouts and loss of privileges throughout the day.*
- *Gabriel laid down, face up on the deck. He pulled xxxxx on top of him so that she was laying face first on top of him. He said "this is how I love you" while bouncing her on top of him.*
- *Urinated in his pants. When I asked him if he peed in his pants he replied, "I am not going to stop playing; I want to pee in my underwear."*
- *Ran in to the corner of the kitchen table (bruised cheek).*
- *Ran into corner of wall and hit nose.*
- *Backed into corner of wall and banged back of head. (Note: there are two other points that are complete fiction and so totally vicious and vile that we have removed them. They do not represent the actions of <u>ANY</u> four-year-old child. They only show the complete depravity of Mrs. Foster.)*

Same day, written by the same person but totally different messages! However, we raised Gabriel from birth and <u>never</u> did he exhibit or even give any hint of that type of behavior. So we didn't believe her second email and see it as simply setting the stage to ask for more CFSA funding. If there is any truth whatsoever to her second email, it is possible that after being forced by CFSA and the Fosters to spend slightly more than two weeks in a foster home occupied by older kids—whom he says abused him—he was getting back at the Fosters. Again, if any of the second transcription is true then everyone can understand why Alberta has so many adults today that were in government care facilities as children who are disturbed to varying degrees. Take a great, compassionate, loving child away from loving family, tell that child innumerable lies, place them in foster care, abuse them psychologically and physically, and although we all know CFSA is completely to blame, it is the children that are psychologically and potentially permanently damaged. Notwithstanding the above, CFSA claims that it is okay because children are resilient. But more to the point, these two messages from Mrs. Foster show the reader the type of person that had custody of our grandson by order of CFSA. Mrs. Foster had no sense of right or wrong as she clearly boasted about enjoying Gabriel even though she kidnapped Gabriel from me. Armed with our newfound interpretations and the real fear and concern that they generated in us, we now redoubled our efforts to get our grandson back. But Mrs. Foster was not finished with her attempts at removing every and/or all family members from Gabriel's life.

The Fosters relocated to a larger house and told CFSA that we were never to learn of their move or to where they had moved. Even after we successfully got a court order to have 10-hour weekly unsupervised visits with Gabriel at our home, Mrs. Foster insisted that CFSA supply a driver to pick up Gabriel at the Foster house and deliver him to our home for 9 a.m. Then a driver would collect Gabriel at our home at 6:30 p.m. to return him to the Fosters. Consider the sheer stupidity and cost of this. We found out that some drivers came from as far as North Calgary, which is an affront to the Alberta taxpayer. We wanted to pick up and deliver Gabriel, but since Mrs. Foster objected and she led the CFSA imbecile parade, this practice carried on for months. Once again, these so-called protectors of children and families greatly contributed to exposing Gabriel to so many strangers, safety risks, and completely removing his ability to trust. However, Mrs. Foster's diabolical antics went even further. In her efforts to completely deprive us of ever seeing our grandson, twice the Fosters took short vacations and left Gabriel with some acquaintances whom we believe also had foster children. We learned this from Gabriel who came to us with chest congestion and severe rash on his arms, neck, and legs. He told us that the Fosters went away and left him with "their friends" who had animals, and he slept in a round bed on the floor, most likely a dog basket bed. On that same stay, Gabriel somehow also lost his much needed eye glasses. The Fosters were doing anything and everything to make sure we did not have access to Gabriel. They knew we wanted Gabriel at any time they would not be able to look after him or if they were unable to take him with them, but they were intent on punishing us because we were now really fighting them and CFSA for custody of our grandson. How could the CFSA ideal family have so little regard for the health of our beautiful, compassionate little grandson? How could anyone be so cruel?

With Melani's help we reviewed CFSA policies and were able to find sections that clearly stated that no apprehensions would or should take place when a relative is willing and able to provide a stable home environment, especially where that relative was also a guardian. In Chapter 5 of the CYFEA Agreements and Orders the Policy section clearly states the following:

Apprehend a child only if:
- the child is in need of intervention per s.1 (2),
- less intrusive measures cannot adequately protect the child, and
- remaining in the current situation will endanger the child's survival, security or development.

On all counts there was no justifiable reason whatsoever to remove Gabriel from us but there was potential justification to remove Gabriel from the Fosters. So what happened? What dirty tricks were CFSA and the Fosters playing?

We had all the proof that we needed to demand that Gabriel be immediately returned to us. Armed with that knowledge we contacted Don Wijesooriya to force his hand and have him explain why his staff broke policy and were so adamant in removing Gabriel from our care. Don's first response was that we were too old and then after considering what he had just said he added that his team felt that Gabriel was with the ideal family. But he never explained why CFSA unlawfully apprehended Gabriel, and he was adamant that Gabriel would not be returned to us. His comments only increased our resolve to rescue Gabriel from such corrupt, uncaring, self-serving people, both within CFSA and the Fosters.

All the while we were fighting with CFSA and the Fosters, we continued our campaign of trying to arrange a meeting with the minister of Human Services, Manmeet Bhullar, but neither he nor his office responded, other than with a form letter, to our letters and emails. Here is my second email to the minister written August 27, 2014. Other letters and emails written over

the next two weeks were also ignored even though we copied
the Premier Jim Prentice and Minister of Justice Jonathan Denis:

> The Honourable Manmeet S Bhullar
>
> Have you investigated yesterday's complaint?
>
> AHS FCS granted us a one hour and twenty minute
> supervised visit with our grandson this AM. We now
> know why they forbid us from seeing our grandson,
> he has drastically changed! He is shy, quiet, very
> unhappy, and we know this has been caused by your
> department and their uncaring attitude toward the
> family. He used to run, joke, be overcome with ques-
> tions, play happily....but he has suffered extensive
> trauma in your so called care.
>
> You know that he should never have been removed
> from loving families, especially in light of the trauma
> experienced with his biological parents. We thought
> we were successfully rehabilitating him, but all that
> work has been undone by your department's incom-
> petence. We are now very angry!
>
> Since I have court ordered "guardianship" and
> "parentship" of my grandson, how can I explain to
> him that I am forbidden from seeing him more often
> than you allow and always with "strangers"? How
> can a 3 ½ year old process this inhumane intrusion
> into what used to be his happy normal life? Please do
> something now!
>
> Respectfully,

This email was also sent to our MLA Danielle Smith but neither the minister nor our MLA had the decency to even acknowledge receipt, never mind reply.

As the end of 2014 approached, we finally found another lawyer, Brendan Miller of Walsh LLP. He asked that for the meeting, following our initial meeting with him, we bring every document, email, letter, etc., that we could find. We brought everything including all our original letters, emails to the various ministers, to CFSA caseworkers, etc., and approximately 340 double-sided handwritten documents representing CFSA documentation of all proceedings, we received from our previous lawyer. As Brendan reviewed our case with us and examined these documents, he kept shaking his head asking both us and himself how an agency of the government can have so much disrespect for the law and their clients. He showed us documents that were clearly fabrications, as well as contradictions in affidavits, and wondered how our case could be so "screwed up." He immediately asked for a judicial dispute resolution (JDR) to try to show any presiding judge the unlawfulness of our case.

In the meantime, we continually fought the Fosters in order to get access to our grandson. Then we inadvertently learned through a CFSA comment at one of our family meetings that Mrs. Foster did not want us to have any access to Gabriel. Now things were becoming clearer. A comment made by Mrs. Foster the second time we babysat their children came to mind that all she needed was access to about $12,000 to $15,000 annually and then she wouldn't need to work. My husband and I looked at each other dumbfounded! She had accomplished her goal. Now all she had to do was bring Jackson onside by encouraging his hatred of me, so we expected her to play up to Jackson, which she did. We watched her in action. Before the apprehension she was out to get Jackson. She collected self-incriminating Facebook postings by Jackson to be given to the RCMP, then she told everyone about a big black truck that was continually driving up her street, suspecting it was Jackson or one of his friends, and she suspected Jackson of taking some children's clothing off her front porch. Suspecting that Jackson had contravened his EPO, she sent the RCMP to check to see if he was with my husband at the condo on August 4, his moving day. Ironically, at that time, my ex was with my husband at the condo getting ready to move out all of Jackson's belongings, and my ex took exception to the RCMP's intrusion and demanded to know why they had come. He learned that Mrs. Foster had sent them. So what next? We didn't have long to wait.

During the period August 2014 to December 2014 we continued to attend court but this time with our lawyer. And CFSA agreed to visitations with Gabriel at our home, usually ranging one and a half hours but still with "approved" supervision. However, one supervisor wrote this email to us for which he got into serious trouble:

> Hi Mr. and Mrs.—Sep 12, 2014
>
> Thank you again for allowing me to supervise such a wonderful visit with you and Gabriel. It's clear that you love Gabriel very much …
>
> Again, thank you and have a great day. signed

This email resulted in CFSA re-examining their requirement for supervising our visits, and it gave our lawyer some ammunition for our upcoming JDR in October 2014. That judge ordered that we be given unsupervised visitations of 10 hours weekly.

It was troubling that the CFSA, with Mrs. Foster's insistence, unilaterally changed visitation from the 9 a.m. to 7 p.m. agreed at during the JDR to 9:30 a.m. to 7 p.m. to once again show us that they were in control and could do whatever they wanted. However, at the next JDR in December my husband told the judge about the CFSA manipulation of the visitation hours and he ordered that we receive a "minimum" of 10 hours per week which immediately came into effect…but CFSA and the Fosters made sure that we did not get even one minute more!

Melani met with us regularly to plan our next moves and to attend family meetings that were arranged by CFSA in their attempts to get all parties to talk to each other. This was an impossible task as the Fosters made it clear they were not interested in any relationship with us. My son couldn't stand being in the same room as me. My husband only attended one session and said that CFSA didn't know what they were doing and he was not going to waste his time with liars and cheats. But the most telling verification of my husband's comment came when John Hoveland, a CFSA supervisor, told my husband that he was going to "make" Jackson get clean and stay clean. My husband asked him how he planned to achieve that goal and he answered, "I've given him a real objective, he either keeps his son or loses him." As if "everyone" had not already warned Jackson many times over! As we left the CFSA office, my husband looked back in John Hoveland's direction and told me that this wet-behind-the-ears lightweight without any addiction experience is so full of himself that he is going to "make" Jackson get and stay clean. What a waste of our time. I had tried for nine years to get Jackson to clean himself up, even going as far as potentially gifting him our condo. My husband who has experience in addiction and anger management counselling tried. Even Jackson's father and

Jackson's sponsor did everything they could, but even though he stayed clean several times, up to two years, he inevitably relapsed. John was just another incompetent pawn in the CFSA system echoing anything his manager wanted him to say. These meetings proved to be a complete waste of time. Nothing of value was ever discussed. My husband proposed a cleaning of the slate, apologies all around, and working only in the best interests of Gabriel, but the Fosters said they would never apologize as they did absolutely nothing wrong. Then my husband, supported by Melani, asked John Hoveland why CFSA had never responded to our email of October 7. But John's answer was just one more lie; he said CFSA did respond but we didn't like the answer. Melani took real exception to his lie and told him there had never been any reply from anyone at CFSA, and to please start telling the truth. But because the truth, for our case, does not exist at CFSA, the meetings were slowly disbanded. A copy of the October 7, 2014 email to which there has been no response to this day follows:

To don.wijesooriya (Manager)
linda.eirikson (Asst Director)
CC heather.klimchuk (Minister Human Services)

Dear Mr. Wijesooriya and Ms. Eirikson,

Although the Initial Custody Order was granted last week, and despite your application for a Permanent Guardianship Order, I understand that your agency has an obligation to still work with our family. We are very concerned that as of yet we have not felt as if your employees have given us any assistance at all, quite the contrary. We feel the need to make a few points clear to you, and as you have denied allowing us to bring our chosen support person to a meeting with you, then we will inform you of these points, & ask questions, by email.

The judge commented last week that he was not sure that CFSA actually had grounds for the apprehension order. An EPO was in place to protect us. We did not feel threatened by Jackson or Janet, the relatives with whom Gabriel had been staying voiced concerns that they were fearful after a phone call with Jackson's father. Why were we not allowed to pick up Gabriel from their home and allow the EPO to protect us as it is designed to do? I am a guardian and would have taken the necessary steps to ensure, as we both have been doing since the EPO was granted, Gabriel's safety. In the affidavit it states that Gabriel was in the vehicle when Jackson assaulted me. This is untrue. Gabriel was at home with my husband. This incident occurred in May, hence the EPO. Why was this grounds for apprehension in August? The RCMP officer also questioned this but when we attempted to discuss this with Shawna Asselstine she commented that this law doesn't apply to CFSA and hung up, ending the conversation. This was not only highly unprofessional but added to our distress. Why weren't less intrusive measures discussed such as a custody agreement if CFSA really believed Gabriel to be in danger and needing to reside elsewhere? Although we still maintain that Gabriel was not in any danger. In the contact notes it clearly states on August 13/14 that the RCMP do not believe that Jackson is a risk. In fact on 7 August/14 Bonita Hoffman-Russel had informed Mrs. Foster that everything was fine and that the file was to be closed. Nothing else occurred, there were no changes to this file other than one phone call that made Mr. and Mrs. Foster feel unsafe, even though the person making the so called threats was many miles away. Mr. and Mrs. Foster did not have to continue to care for Gabriel and could have dealt with their feelings of fear quite apart from us.

Why after the apprehension were we not allowed any access to Gabriel? We had to wait for three weeks until we could see him. We felt extremely distressed so we can only imagine how Gabriel felt being placed in a foster home with no contact with the people who loved him and had been caring for him.

Although we have limited access to Gabriel now we have many concerns about his well-being in the home of Mr. and Mrs. Foster. If your mandate is truly to ensure the children's needs are considered why has Gabriel had to change his pre-school program? His place has been paid for at Okotoks Montessori, he is still living in this community and he would have benefited greatly from the consistency. We have not been told where Gabriel is going to pre-school now and have no information on the program. We are requesting that he return to Montessori immediately. Why has his doctor been changed? He has a family doctor in Black Diamond. Has he had any medical appointments since being apprehended, as we have not been notified of any. We have been told by the case worker that we are not allowed to go and watch Gabriel in his community activities such as gymnastics. Why has this decision been made? Why is he being transported to his visits with us by an agency, having to meet different drivers every week? Not only is this an unnecessary cost to the government, it is not in Gabriel's best interest when we are more than willing and able to pick him up at Foster residence. We are not a threat to them in any way and would have hoped that they would have seen the benefit of working with us in Gabriel's best interest. This does not appear to be the case. We would like this changed immediately and either have Mrs. Foster drive him to our home or we will collect him.

Although my mental health is in question we would like to make it clear to you that I have never had any mental health issues in the past; the doctor at the South Calgary Health Campus assessed me as fit and well other than situational distress. My husband does admit to sending an email to Mrs. Foster that was a fabrication. He did this in an attempt to make her understand how devastated I was. I never took an overdose or spoke of suicide and my husband understands how this could be misconstrued. He obviously regrets using this method as a way of attempting to make Mr. and Mrs. Foster understand how devastated we both felt and would have been happy to discuss this with your staff but were not asked or given an opportunity to do so.

We are able to assess risk. Last Christmas Jackson and Janet were angry with us for, in their opinion, withholding Gabriel from them. Jackson had not used for a period of 5+ days, Janet was sober and Jackson's sponsor was with them. We made the reasoned decision to allow Gabriel to spend time with them. We are diligent in not allowing Gabriel access to his parents if they have been using drugs. We are both well aware of the signs of drug use and able to effectively protect Gabriel and have attended Al-an-on to gain first-hand knowledge of drug users.

As we are both older we had been exploring options that may be able to assist us in parenting Gabriel if he was to stay with us long term. As this was looking more likely with his parents unable to maintain sobriety we had been in discussion with Mr. and Mrs. Foster about how they might be able to assist. We were being pro-active in our planning and we had mentioned this both to CFSA and Gabriel's lawyer. This was then assumed to mean that we could no longer care for him now. That is not the case. Please see the safety plan below.

As our lawyer has now finished working with us we have the disclosure package. It is very concerning on many fronts. Bonita Hoffman-Russel's handwriting is so illegible for the most part that it makes the contact notes almost impossible to read, even with a magnifying glass. Please review the file and let us know your thoughts. As your notes, Mr. Wijesooriya, are typed are we to assume that this is actually how contact notes should be recorded? On 25 August there is an email sent to us from Mrs. Foster telling us how well Gabriel is doing with examples, yet on the same day there is a contact note written from a phone call between the worker and Mrs. Foster which is absolutely opposite. Please review and explain what this might mean. We will send you our e mail for the purpose of referencing. The filing appears to be completely out of date order making the whole disclosure package very difficult to read or make sense of.

As part of our desire to ensure Gabriel's safety we attended at Rowan House Emergency Women's Shelter and had a meeting to go over how we intended to protect our family. The worker told us that we had done everything possible apart from inform our neighbors. We did so upon our return home.

No services have been offered to us to alleviate the perceived risk factors. What services will you be offering? What will be their goals?

No safety mapping meeting has been arranged as per your social work model, Signs of Safety. When will this occur? We have many friends, family and professionals who are able to attest that Gabriel is not at risk and who would be willing and able to report any concerns to CFSA should any arise.

SAFETY PLAN

EPO is in place until January 2015

A full time live-in nanny will be hired to assist in day to day care of Gabriel. All visitation with the parents will be supervised by either an agency or the Safe Visitation Program

A list of family and friends will be provided to CFSA to show the support system that exists for us.

As my computer capability is limited I will forward another e-mail with important attachments that further attest to our concern over what is truth and what is fiction.

Yours truly,

Although the above email was copied and sent the next day to Associate Director Christina Tortorelli, she ignored our efforts at communication and never replied, even to this day. Many of the issues covered earlier in this chapter were specifically addressed in our email as we and our lawyer felt that the evidence was irrefutably in our favor. But no response from anyone in the system clearly highlights the level of incompetence, corruption, cover-ups, complete lack of concern for our grandson and our family, and the abuse being heaped on our grandson by CFSA and their "ideal" family, the Fosters. The abuse by CFSA being hurled against us became oppressive and brought to light how powerless individuals really are against government corruption reaching all the way up to incompetent judges.

Can you imagine the judge at the JDR identifying that he did not believe that CFSA had sufficient grounds for apprehending Gabriel, but refusing to correct the unlawful act and recommending that the case proceed to trial. Just more horrific costs for us!

All he needed to do was to check the written affidavit by CFSA's Bonita Hoffman-Russell at the beginning of the Permanent Guardianship Order (unfortunately this document has not been returned to us by our lawyer even though it is our property) that attested to the quality care we had provided to Gabriel and ask us some direct questions to satisfy himself that we were ready and able to continue to care for Gabriel. Instead, he chose to allow the unlawful acts of CFSA to prevail and thereby continue the terrible abuse to Gabriel. What was he thinking? Even with Jackson's tirade against me, the judge should have been astute enough to know that Jackson's words were from a drug-fried brain. He of all people should have known how unreliable statements made by a practicing addict really are. He was not invested in our case and therefore lacked any real concern for our grandson; period. Was he possibly influenced by, or in the control of the director of Child and Family Services as the CYFEA bestows so much power to that position? He also should have used information from the disclosure documents together with his "judgement" to give appropriate weight to the claims made by Gabriel's parents. Most people (including lawyers, family members, and friends) knew that almost every time Jackson and Janet opened their mouths lies flowed out; it was the drugs talking! We have attended court hearings where judges "considered" statements by hard-core addicts as self-serving, without a moral compass, or that they would say or do anything to get their way. But this judge seemed oblivious. So my husband reminded me of a consulting assignment he had undertaken as the expert witness for a large Calgary law firm on behalf of the provincial judges back in 1998–1999. He had tried to get the government to move from a typical union system, same pay for all judges, to more of a merit or performance pay system as he identified that some judges were merely "putting in time" (and should be forced to retire) and others were significantly underpaid compared to their level of experience, judgement, and quality of work performance. Can you guess what category this judge falls into? I hold him responsible for sanctioning the continued abuse to my grandson and robbing us of much needed retirement funds.

As a follow-up to the JDR with this disappointment of a judge trial dates were set as follows:

- March 30 and 31, 2015
- One half day April 1, 2015
- April 2, 7, 8 and half day on April 9, 2015
- With a pretrial conference scheduled for January 8, 2015 and a second JDR set for December 2, 2014.

The family meetings referenced earlier were started by CFSA in an attempt to get all parties to try to work for the best interests of Gabriel, but Jackson wanted Gabriel returned to him, we wanted Gabriel returned to our custody, and CFSA and the Fosters had already agreed among themselves that the Fosters were the chosen family. You didn't need to be a genius to see through the setup. It is no wonder that the "family" meetings failed; besides these meetings were hosted by very incompetent people that clearly had predetermined outcomes.

We continued to petition the minister of Human Services although there was never any reply, just form letters. Furthermore, our MLA Danielle Smith dodged us and was completely successful at never meeting with us or even providing one ounce of help. She simply didn't care. Then when she committed the ultimate betrayal of switching from the Wildrose party to the Alberta Progressive Conservative party (the party in government at that time whose policies she said she vehemently opposed) and supporting their policies, we knew! She had no concern for her constituents; she was looking after herself. Therefore, how could she rock the boat with the department of Human Services? She was clearly in a conflict of interests.

CFSA and the Fosters conspired to withhold any information that we should have had access to, and in one very important case we inadvertently learned that "they" were allowing Jackson and his new girlfriend to have supervised access to Gabriel. These are the same people that removed Gabriel from our custody due to CFSA and the Fosters claiming that Jackson posed a lethal threat to not only Gabriel but to the Fosters as well. What changed?

We surmise that Mrs. Foster needed an ally against us and since Jackson was in a very compromised state and very susceptible to anything or anyone that seemed to be an ally, she used him. And as it was she and CFSA that had forbidden him to have any contact with Gabriel, the Fosters, or even the Town of Okotoks, he quickly supported them. Perhaps CFSA and the Fosters were realizing that Gabriel wanted or needed his dad, or that they had no grounds to continually block Gabriel's access to his dad. In any event, no documented proof ever surfaced to support their claims of Jackson posing a lethal threat to Gabriel or the Fosters. And even more remote was the potential lethal threat to us or our property, as we so vociferously pointed out on August 8, 2014 when we tried unsuccessfully to stop the illegal apprehension of Gabriel.

Slowly we learned that the Fosters, with the support of CFSA, were allowing Jackson and his girlfriend to have increasing supervised access to Gabriel; Mrs. Foster's attempt at befriending Jackson in order to have another ally against me was working. A service from Lethbridge was hired by CFSA to provide "professional" oversight and supervision whenever the Fosters allowed Jackson and his girlfriend visitation with Gabriel. Then as Christmas approached, we felt very strongly that Gabriel should spend Christmas with family. So we asked Jessica both by email and voice mail for access to Gabriel on December 25 and also January 1. Her reply by voice mail was "NO." We immediately contacted the department manager Don Wijesooriya for his intervention. Once again, he declined to act which required us to file another administrative review request. He then immediately responded by phone scolding us and telling us that he would not allow the administrative review on the basis that we never got a "decision" to our request for Christmas visitation with Gabriel. However, to Don W's surprise, when my husband played back Jessica's voice mail message which sounded very decisive, Don W fumbled around for an answer and then said that she could not make that decision, therefore she was simply communicating their "plan." Melani, who was in our living room with us at the time, as our resource could not believe how anyone could be so slippery and evasive; my more appropriate description is "slimy." Anyway, the result was that Don would block any attempt to have an AR request, which he did by ruling that the "director" had the jurisdiction to rule that we could not challenge Don's decision. But wait! We did receive a phone reply to our AR request, from Bev Fournier, manager, advising us that our request for Christmas visitation with Gabriel was denied because they ruled that Gabriel needed to be quiet and in an unthreatening environment. Ironically, at the time of her phone call, Gabriel was sitting on my husband's lap listening to a story that my husband was reading. So, I mentioned this to Bev Fournier and asked her what could be more quiet and unthreatening. And I reminded her that Gabriel was competing with three other kids, one of whom he did not like, and was away from his family; what makes that situation so desirable? And one week later we received an email from Bev Fournier and Pat Gilbert confirming their decision that Gabriel needed to spend time with his dad and the Fosters. Strange ruling, considering that Jackson was previously considered "dangerous" by CFSA, or was there total collusion? Their review was so fictitious and so phony, in our opinion, as the information that they communicated was wrong; they wrote that they knew we would have Gabriel January 2, 2015 but December 31, 2014 was our last scheduled day. But even more disconcerting is that during their so-called investigation they only spoke with John Hoveland, team leader, who reports to Don Wijesooriya and to Don Wijesooriya himself. What kind of review is that? Once again the manipulations continued with no realistic reasons ever given for CFSA decisions. And here begins another roadblock to any justice or fairness.

With Melani's help we filed an objection to Don W's blocking of the request for administrative review and we also challenged the decision from Bev Fournier and Pat Gilbert. That resulted in a request from Sofia Guichon, a representative of CYFE, for us to complete a "challenge to the director's decision," which we did. But once we read all of the conditions under which a challenge could succeed we decided not to pursue the challenge. The act once again makes it virtually impossible to challenge anything undertaken in the director's name. Section 120 (2) lays out exactly what is challengeable, which is virtually nothing. Here is just one example of stacking the deck against anyone challenging the director. First, the administrative review is undertaken not by independent personnel but rather by "managers" or "associate directors" of CFSA Calgary region. Wow! Is it any wonder that we lost every request? Colleagues assessing the work of colleagues in the same region and this government believes decisions should be credible, or do they? Now we were being reassured that this challenge will be decided by an independent committee under the auspices of the Appeals Secretariat of Alberta Human Services. Remember that we requested access to our grandson for December 24 and 25 and January 1. We were now into March; both Christmas Day and New Year's Day had long passed, so Don W and the Fosters once again rob us and our grandson of family time. Oh, by April 17 we received the panel's final decision advising us that the director's decision was not challengeable. What a farce! Does this ever smack of a government that is so corrupt that any potential obstacle is ruled inadmissible? These people are worse than criminals.

I don't know who or what the director of Child and Family Services is, but I do know that in our case only evil, hurtful decisions have been made by that position, every single one dedicated to winning at all costs and mostly at the expense of the CFSA client (our grandson). In summary, my husband and I believe that the director position has deteriorated from its originally designed intent to the point of acting as a piece of human garbage and being represented in that manner as evidenced above by Don Wijesooria, as well as by lawyers, and other CFSA representatives.

Now that we were seeing Gabriel, unsupervised, for 10 hours every week he was starting to tell us more of what he was going through. Sometimes he made off-the-cuff comments, like, "I can't spend more time with you because you have to be better" or "Grandma, I can't call Grandma and Papa's house home because Mrs. Foster says I can't live here, ever" and "Mrs. Foster says I can never stay with daddy Jackson, I can only visit him." Gabriel collected his thoughts one day and told us about the Fosters taking the family shopping, but because they said he misbehaved they would not take him into the store, so they locked him in the car *alone*. He became so scared that he tried to get out but a very loud alarm and horns came on. Then one day I showed Gabriel the bathtub bubble maker that I wanted very much to use whenever he stayed long enough for a bath, and he wanted me to turn it on. I told him that we would definitely turn it on when he is here for his bath. Gabriel responded "But Grandma, I can't because I am not safe here! The judge says it's not safe." He then quietly said "you know Mrs. Foster loves me," and breaks down and cries. So I tried to reassure him that he is very safe here and then Gabriel cried and told us that he really loved us. Can you believe that adult foster babysitters just keep poisoning a four-year-old innocent little boy and they continue to be promoted and protected by CFSA? Those comments by Gabriel were innocently made without any prompting. We wonder how much additional poisoning of family he was forced to listen to? Even with us forwarding these comments to CFSA and the minister, absolutely no action was taken. However, the Fosters must have realized that we were slowly finding out about their abusive actions as they took special care to avoid any locations where they might possibly run into us. This avoidance went as far as Mrs. Foster not attending her daughter's Christmas pageant at play school (even though Mrs. Foster unilaterally changed Gabriel's preschool from Okotoks Montessori to Mrs. Foster's preferred play school) because we learned from Gabriel's teacher, at the new play school, that we could and should attend the same Christmas pageant for Gabriel, which we did.

Perhaps I need to bring forward some actual case details so that readers that have familiarity with CFSA processes can see specifically what was happening to us and our grandson. The reference, in our email of October 7, 2014, to a PGO being applied for by CFSA, was CFSA's way of gaining total and complete control of Gabriel. Every lawyer and every resource person we spoke to strongly advised and insisted that we fight that order with every tool available to us. Because, once CFSA were to be granted the PGO they could send Gabriel to whomever and wherever they chose. They could allow the Fosters to adopt Gabriel without any regard for family opposition if they chose that course. And then Gabriel's real family would be totally shut out of his life. So, we fought that order in court and limited CFSA to an Interim Guardianship Order although they continued to petition the court for a PGO. But at every step another obstacle arises.

The court appointed a "legal representative" for Gabriel, supposedly to protect his interests. His lawyer was Margaret Bodeux-Tang and her first appearance in court tells us that the deck is stacked even more against us. Without any real interview of me and without ever speaking to my husband, she wrote to the judge indicating that I said I could not parent Gabriel and that I was spiteful because I didn't want the Fosters to have Gabriel. First, my husband and I co-parent, and my husband would have set her straight if she had bothered to talk to him. She wrote very <u>emphatic negative comments</u> without factual support and when asked by the judge if she had seen Gabriel, she answered, not yet! As far as we know, and even after checking with Gabriel, we believe she most likely has <u>not ever</u> seen or spoken to Gabriel to this day, yet she insisted that the judge not return Gabriel to us as we needed to prove competence to parent Gabriel. Obviously, she did not review the file or she completely "missed" Bonita's comments of our exemplary parenting, or she was simply doing what she was told by the director's staff. So, once again the CYFEA provides just one more obstacle to guardians trying to help their children and grandchildren. But this time an inferior, poorly thought out act is further deprived of any value by a lawyer that willfully manipulates the system for her benefit, not her client's benefit. More about Bodeux-Tang in a later chapter. She is just one more pawn for use by CFSA caseworkers and the "omnipotent" director.

As we met occasionally with our lawyer to prepare for the upcoming trial, our lawyer learned, after the JDR of December 2, 2014, that the trial dates had been set back to November 2, 3, 5, 9, 10, and 12, 2015. Although my husband and I became even more disgusted with our "justice" (sorry "legal") system, this delay actually worked to our benefit in the long run. But Gabriel had to suffer through almost seven more months of abuse. This delay allowed our lawyer to use the extra time to preempt further character assassinations by Child and Family Services by encouraging us to undertake psychological and parenting evaluations.

Since we were not abandoning our fight against CFSA, and that was now clear to everyone, so, with Bodeux-Tang's support, we believe that they (CFSA and Bodeux-Tang) determined to find other means at their disposal to "bury" us. Through our lawyer they "recommended" that we undertake psychological counselling through one of their psychologists and at their cost. Our lawyer strongly suggested that we do so to remove any potential for CFSA or Bodeux-Tang to find us uncooperative, even though we were sure that we did not need any psychological assistance. Since more than one year had passed since we started our requests, followed by demands, that Gabriel be allowed to see a child psychologist (play therapist), we felt this could be the opportunity to also help Gabriel. It was clear that this was more about our ability to parent rather than to help the one who was most vulnerable in this situation. Our psychologist was professional and seemed interested in factual information which put us somewhat at ease.

We filled out numerous pages of questions and answers and attended approximately eight two-hour sessions and then were asked to obtain "reference" letters from people who knew us and had seen us parent Gabriel. That exercise probably helped us more than we could imagine. The psychologist, Dr. Sally During, determined that we were normal, had very good judgement and proven parenting skills, cared for and loved Gabriel unconditionally, but were extremely distraught and frustrated by CFSA and their dirty "tactics." She even recommended that all communication with CFSA be in writing, something that we had tried to implement almost one year earlier but without success. CFSA completely refused to put anything in writing, going as far as ignoring any of our written correspondence or emails. And she wrote in her report that she could find no reason to recommend withholding Gabriel from our custody. The "reference" letters along with the psychologist's report had a strong and very positive impact. Our lawyer now felt that the obstacles created by CFSA and Bodeux-Tang had been demolished and both parties no longer had any ammunition with which to fight us. We continued to demand psychological help for Gabriel. We seemed to be the only ones that could see his pain and knew that he suffered extreme trauma at the hands of CFSA and the Fosters. Even though we were prepared to pay for the services of a play therapist, both CFSA and the Fosters opposed us. They unilaterally decided what they wanted for Gabriel.

In the interim period, Jackson and his new girlfriend Amber were permitted to have a supervised visit with Gabriel that took place at the Calgary Zoo, which the Fosters attended as well. We don't know what happened on that occasion, but immediately thereafter Mrs. Foster advised Jackson by email that she would no longer support any further visitations from Jackson to see his son, and did not want Jackson to have any further contact with her family. She also advised CFSA that she could no longer support Jackson and wanted no further contact with him. She must have learned that our case for regaining custody of Gabriel was improving so she didn't need to be nice to Jackson any longer since being nice to him was an "acting" role that she didn't want anyway. But she miscalculated the damage she caused to herself, especially as she represented "the ideal family" in CFSA's views.

Following the release of the psychologist's report, CFSA approached our lawyer in September 2015 to advise that they were taking their petition for a PGO off the table and would support us in petitioning for a Guardianship and Parenting Order. We did not know about CFSA and the Fosters falling out, but the result of the fallout was that CFSA would no longer support the Fosters as the ideal foster family. What happened to the CFSA ideal family? But Mrs. Foster's true colors came through once more when she was asked by CFSA to assist in transitioning Gabriel back to us if the court granted our Guardianship Order. According to CFSA she wanted no further contact whatsoever with Gabriel if we were granted our order and NO she would not help! Wow, doesn't that action say so much about Mrs. Foster?

CHAPTER 3

The Tide Begins to Turn

Jessica Smith, Gabriel's caseworker, visited with us to advise that CFSA was prepared to support us to obtain guardianship and parentship of Gabriel, but that Margaret Bodeux-Tang still felt that Gabriel should not be moved from the Fosters until all her questions about our ability to parent Gabriel were addressed. Strange that she completely presumed, without any checking, that the Fosters were quite OK to have custody of our grandson but we were not. Lawyers should have some level of intelligence or conscience, but Bodeux-Tang exhibited absolutely none. How could she insist that Gabriel remain in the "care" of the Fosters who did not undertake any testing and were proving completely incapable of providing a safe, loving environment for Gabriel? When a lawyer seems to be only concerned with her fee she does not do the required due diligence and makes and presents unsubstantiated comments as pure fact. Remember that our review of disclosure documents provided us with proof positive of fabricated information by CFSA that was presented as fact and now Bodeux-Tang was doing the same thing. Her lack of professionalism also extended to twice committing to agreed-upon court dates and then not showing up resulting in a postponement and many hundreds of extra dollars in cost for us.

Especially disconcerting was the fact that one of her excuses was that she was on vacation, even though she had previously committed in court to the judge to be present. Bodeux-Tang insisted that we be required to prove our competence to look after our grandson for nine more months before she would agree to Gabriel being returned to us. Yes, nine more months of Bodeux-Tang-imposed trauma for our grandson. What about the abuse he was enduring in foster care? Thank God that at our next court appearance Judge Lipton had done his homework, saw through her antics, and ruled that Gabriel be immediately returned to us at the end of court on October 28 and our guardianship would be reviewed in six months, April 2016.

Since we always said that we would do anything to rescue Gabriel, we discussed with Jessica what else we could do. She volunteered that Margaret Bodeux-Tang needed further third-party proof such as more psychological opinions in order for her to give her approval. And we agreed to see Dr. Roslyn Mendelson a registered psychologist and play therapist around mid-September 2015, only 13 months after we had begged, demanded, etc., CFSA to be allowed to take Gabriel to a play therapist. If we had custody of Gabriel we would simply have done it on our own and at our cost, but that option was never available. Although these appointments were for us, not Gabriel, we felt somewhat reassured that we could also get Dr. Mendelson to eventually see Gabriel.

Since two court dates were chosen to review our petition for guardianship and parentship, October 28 and November 3, 2015, and we had already "won" our Guardianship Order on October 28, we needed finalization of the process on November 3. This time CFSA were actually supporting us. Since September, CFSA had started allowing us to have access to Gabriel more often; twice weekly and on one occasion three times during one week with a sleepover on one occasion. Whenever we met people who knew us and had known Gabriel, we were inevitably asked what was wrong with Gabriel. The scariest incident took place at our friends' home in High River. When we were raising Gabriel one and a half to two years earlier, every time we visited Dennis and Denice, Gabriel would go to the basement with Dennis and bring toys upstairs. Then he would go into the kitchen and go through cupboards looking for funnels, salad spinners, etc. However, on this visit as Denice came up from the basement, Gabriel became terrified, grabbed me and hid behind me. Both Dennis and Denice wondered what was wrong with Gabriel. He had really changed. The trauma that CFSA and the Fosters subjected him to had significantly changed his demeanor, actually his entire personality. He avoided eye contact, rarely smiled, was timid, and trusted no one. He was simply "blank." So as we met with Dr. Mendelson throughout September and October 2015 we normally brought up Gabriel and pleaded that she visit with him. Because Dr. Mendelson is a very caring and professional person and was able to see our pain as a result of the trauma to Gabriel, she petitioned CFSA to be allowed to visit with Gabriel. Her petition of CFSA actually bore fruit in November 2015. However, until October 28, 2015 while Gabriel was still living with the Fosters and thanks to the antics of Bodeux-Tang, the Fosters continued to fight us at every opportunity. Notwithstanding the interference from the Fosters, CFSA allowed us to register Gabriel at the Okotoks Montessori preschool and to see Dr. Mendelson. To continue to make everything as difficult as possible for us, the Fosters refused to take Gabriel to preschool, requiring CFSA to arrange for a driver to pick him up and deliver him to preschool and then collect him from preschool to return him to the Fosters. Remember, that until October 28, 2015 we still had Gabriel for only10 hours on Wednesdays. Also remember that the Fosters did not want us to ever know where they lived, so even though we would have been extremely happy to pick up and deliver Gabriel, the Fosters saw to it that we were not allowed. The joke, if you can call it that, is that we knew where the Fosters were relocating approximately seven or eight days before they actually moved in. Okotoks is a small community and my husband knows many people and has as many acquaintances. If the Fosters felt comfortable and "safer" believing we did not know where they lived, we decided to keep it that way.

CFSA supported us in court and on October 28, 2015, Judge Lipton granted us guardianship as well as parentship of Gabriel even though Bodeux-Tang had requested an additional nine-month assessment period. At the end of court, CFSA told us that they would arrange to have Gabriel at our home within hours, after the end of preschool. Ironically, Jessica Smith committed to pick up Gabriel after school and deliver him to our home as contracting a driver could not be done within the required time frame. At 2:45 p.m. we received a call from the Montessori school telling us that Gabriel was still there and nobody had picked him up. We therefore happily and immediately rushed to the school to pick up our grandson. We returned to court on November 3 to finalize the Guardianship and Parentship Orders. Finally, Gabriel was legally home!

A word here about judges. Four judges, Judge O'Gorman, Judge Lipton, Judge Cornfeild, and Judge LaRochelle are a real credit to the Alberta Court system. They had read and studied the file and were not at all intimidated by the CYFE Act. They actually worked for the child; in this case, our grandson. Had we not been fortunate enough to be in Judge Lipton's court on October 28, 2015, we might still be fighting our case. Unfortunately, we only encountered these four credible, objective judges during our two-year-plus ordeal.

CFSA prepared summaries showing the status of required undertakings and completed commitments for Jackson, Janet, and us. Although we had undertaken and completed our entire list of requirements, unfortunately none of the undertakings had been completed by either Jackson or Janet. So, CFSA continued their requirement that both Jackson and Janet could only have access to Gabriel if the visitation was supervised. But CFSA agreed with us that Jackson should now be allowed back into Okotoks in order to facilitate visits with his son. Therefore, CFSA changed their position concerning Jackson and were prepared to support his freedom to move around within Okotoks. Remember that CFSA were adamant only 16 months earlier, that Jackson posed a lethal threat to Gabriel, my husband, and me. What had now changed? Or were we correct in our assumptions that Bonita's claims were fictitious and self-serving? They also supported a Supervision Order which gave me the responsibility to supervise visits between Gabriel and Jackson. To support this move I attended the Court of Queen's Bench to request that the EPO on Jackson be removed. Both the prosecutor and judge were sympathetic and approved my request. With this additional flexibility we felt that Jackson would feel better about seeing his son. And for a while we were correct, but Jackson did not want any restraints, especially my supervision, and soon started to rebel.

Jackson often challenged my parenting approach. He likes to be assertive (or aggressive) when dealing with Gabriel and feels that I am too soft. On the other hand, my husband and I feel

Jackson, at times, verges on being abusive. There was an unfortunate event early in 2016, just after a night of freezing rain when Jackson came to visit Gabriel while my husband was in High River. He erupted as soon as he entered the house, yelling that he or his girlfriend could have broken their back or a leg because we had not cleared the ice on our steps. Then in his angry mood, he went down to our family room to see Gabriel. But Gabriel was watching TV and didn't immediately acknowledge him which caused another eruption. I immediately went downstairs to warn Jackson to tone down. Once again, he erupted and in front of Gabriel told me that I was not to interfere when he is chastising his son. At this point he was almost physically challenging me, again in view of Gabriel. Since we (all guardians) committed to no arguing, no swearing, no abusive language, no violence, etc. in front of Gabriel, I immediately went upstairs but he followed me and was committed to getting his way. Just then my husband entered the house, saw what was happening, and told Jackson to either cool down or get out. However, Jackson was not finished, he again went downstairs and shaking his finger at Gabriel shouted "your grandma and papa went to court to steal you from me, remember that." He came back upstairs, swore at my husband, and then tried to stop me from going to a neighbor's house.

Now back to the list of commitments, which all guardians agreed to, as prepared by CFSA. Jackson and Janet were required to undertake and prove successful completion of addiction recovery and rehabilitation programs. Both also had to commit to periodic hair follicle tests. As far as we know, little or nothing has been achieved as yet. Jackson was also required to undertake and prove successful completion of anger management programs. The need for anger management now becomes self-evident. How can I trust Jackson to care for Gabriel when he is a ticking time bomb? Both parents do not realize the trauma that Gabriel has been through, and in the event that he can be returned to both or either of them he must have a healthy, unthreatening, stable, and loving environment to live in. But so far, neither parent has undertaken and/or proven successful completion of the required programs. Unfortunately, or in this particular case it may prove positive that Gabriel has little or no recollection of his mother, so whether or not she undertakes the CFSA mandated requirements now seems irrelevant.

My husband convinced me to share our thoughts of Jackson's issues and actions with my ex, Trevor. He felt that if Jackson learned that a united front, consisting of Trevor, my husband, and me, had the same concerns about him and we were all prepared to help Jackson, he just might undertake the required work. However, that was a waste of time as my ex does not see Jackson's issues and does not believe that the programs are really necessary, especially the anger management issues. Jackson seems convinced that I am the cause of most of his problems. With my ex reinforcing Jackson's behavior and actions, the likelihood of Jackson committing to completing any of the required programs is very remote. And it doesn't seem to matter that these programs and proof of successful accomplishment is a court mandated requirement before either parent can be considered fit enough to parent Gabriel.

One more piece to Jackson's freezing rain eruption that has really hurt him is the fact that when he left our home, he immediately drove to the RCMP in High River to report me for assault. Since the RCMP has quite a file on him they phoned both my husband and me to learn exactly what happened. More importantly, Jackson's behavior and actions were reported to CFSA which resulted in CFSA instructing me to not have further contact with Jackson. Jackson was then required to have either my ex or a professional service present to supervise visits between him and Gabriel. Why do some people insist on becoming their own worst enemy? And here is more irony! Jackson feels comfortable with my husband supervising his visitations and has been rather conciliatory. But with my husband's physical disabilities he can only do so for short periods. Trying to pave the way for Jackson to see Gabriel, I contacted Family Ties in High River. They provide no-fee service for parent visitations, but Jackson just rebelled and said that nobody stops him from seeing his son; he doesn't need Family Ties!

As I think back to Jackson's childhood I see a great disconnect. He used to bring home stray animals, even kids who were locked out of their homes, ask me to feed them, look after them, etc. There is a photo on our fridge taken approximately six or seven years ago of Jackson sitting in our pasture with a horse lying beside him, resting his head on Jackson. Where has my son gone?

Jackson is a real dichotomy. He is probably the most personable of all our sons. He is very technologically and mechanically inclined, a real self-starter, and strong as an ox. He had and continues to have a real concern for people, yet he can lose it so quickly at times. We know he loves his son and shows it almost always; but it's the few times when he loses it that worry us. We constantly wrestle with finding a way to make those events less and less.

Just in time to refocus us on the positives, we receive an email from Dr. Roslyn Mendelson to report that she has received CFSA approval to see Gabriel; yes! On our first visit with Dr. Roslyn she quickly analyzes that Gabriel is "flat." He is just going through the motions but he lacks any type of personality. He will not, and probably cannot, talk about his feelings. There is much work to be done.

CHAPTER 4

Life with Gabriel

Having seen the complete shutdown of Gabriel while we had him one day per week we expected a significant adjustment and rehabilitation period. He was not the same boy we had raised. He refused to ever talk about "the other house" and whenever he did it was easy to see his anger and his fear. CFSA delivered several boxes of his belongings to us just days after the court granted guardianship on October 28. Although we expected him to be happy and to delve into these boxes, he didn't really give them much attention. He had toys in his room and he now had *his own* room.

Slowly we found out from Gabriel that the boxes of "toys" that CFSA delivered to us were not really his favorite toys, and according to him some were junk. He wanted the toys that we had given the Fosters for him when we were trying to minimize the trauma of his move to their house. He also remembered and wanted his own bed (the convertible bed). In order to retrieve Gabriel's preferred toys and furniture we asked Jessica to retrieve these from the Fosters. But the impossible took place! The Fosters said that everything requested had disappeared and they could not locate anything. So the heirloom toys that Gabriel and my two sons placed so much attachment and value to have now "vanished" without explanation according to Mrs. Foster. How can potential adoptive parents think so little of their prospective child that they don't return any of his property and belongings?

But in contrast to the Fosters we got great support from Sharlene Brown, Gabriel's Montessori preschool teacher. She continually monitored Gabriel's scholastic performance as well as his social skills and how he interacted with his classmates. Gabriel looked forward to school every Tuesday, Wednesday, and Thursday. We also noticed that he participated in school activities whereas in his previous school he seemed to just coast along. We tried to find things to do on non-school days as he needed some challenges and friendships with children his age. He particularly enjoyed visiting the Nanton Air Museum, the Nanton Garden Train and Store, and Heritage Park. Nevertheless, he wanted kids most of all. And thanks to many of our friends who are also grandparents with grandkids in the same age range as Gabriel, we have been able to accommodate him.

When we had Gabriel, before he was apprehended by CFSA, we had routines that he had become accustomed to, like mealtime, bath time, bed time, story time, etc. Now everything needed to be relearned. Gabriel used to eat everything on his plate and even if he didn't like something, he would at least try it. However, his habits had changed and definitely not for the better. My husband, who does most of the cooking, asked Gabriel to help him one day, and that was a hit. Gabriel, now five years old, was helping Papa make poached eggs, pasta sauce, cappuccino, and KD, yes KD! And this seemed to perk his interest in being back home. He started to ask Papa to push him on his swing, for a "cold" dessert after finishing his supper, to ride the tractor, or to feed the birds. He also remembered his bath, the occasional Jacuzzi, and his bubble maker. He was very slowly returning to his old self, but he seemed afraid of something. It came to light at night; he needed his Papa to sit in Papa's chair in the living room and watch over him until he fell asleep. But he could not tell us what was bothering him or what he feared. He didn't know!

Dr. Roslyn told us that she would try to find out what was bothering him. So in play therapy she was able to determine that he perceived some evil, but he would always shut down before elaborating. Dr. Roslyn did, however, win his trust and he slowly became more forthcoming, but something in his past was evil and buried deeply in his mind. He nevertheless saw Dr. Roslyn as a friend and actually looked forward to his sessions. Then one day as my husband was driving Gabriel to preschool, Gabriel volunteered that he was afraid that someone would break in at night and take him. That is why he needed Papa to protect him at night. We tried to reassure him that our home was very secure and that no one could break in, but he said "they" will go into the garage and get a chainsaw and break into the house. And whatever we tell him does not help because "they took me already." So my husband continues to sit in his chair in the living room to watch over him when he goes to bed until he falls asleep. Hopefully Dr. Mendelson will eventually find the cause of Gabriel's angst and my husband can then watch some night-time TV.

It has been almost 16 months since Gabriel has been in our care and we definitely see huge improvement in his personality. He now even teases us the odd time. Sharlene Brown was so happy just recently when Gabriel laughed out loud in class. This was the first time he showed outward emotion in school. Dr. Roslyn told us to expect some of the usual five-year-old attitude, but although Gabriel does have some "bad" days he has been and continues to be a real blessing. His compassionate attitude is returning; he likes helping out, and wants desperately to go on a camping trip. But there is still a long road ahead.

Gabriel worships his dad and looks forward to anytime that he and his dad can get together. As we previously stated, we firmly believe in the family unit: mother, father, and son. With all the joy comes great risk every so often, and Gabriel has already seen too much heartache in his young life. Without Trevor recognizing that Jackson is a functioning addict, and a very volatile person who desperately needs help and could easily harm his son, although not intentionally, we cannot offer Jackson a tough love scenario, where we support him as he spends all the time needed for complete rehabilitation and to enroll in and graduate from really effective anger management programs. Until July 28, 2016, CFSA has assumed that role but their involvement has now ended. We wish that we could get Jackson and his father to recognize that raising Gabriel is not about trying to create another Jackson with Jackson thoughts, Jackson drive, Jackson strength; it's about raising a beautiful little boy who needs tender loving care. However, this can't be done by imposing Jackson's will on Gabriel. To further attest to Jackson's resistance to everything, he has objected to Gabriel continuing to see Dr. Mendelson, forcing us to seek a court order to clearly specify my role. More importantly his interference hurts his son, especially as Dr. Mendelson and Gabriel had developed a "real" trust relationship and both my husband and I were feeling that she was on the verge of a possible breakthrough. So does Jackson really love his son or is everything really about Jackson?

Over the winter of 2015–2016 Gabriel was in Timbits hockey which he just loved; but the attraction was the kids. Although he was far from being the best player, he never missed a practice or a game; or even thought of not going. We were really blessed as his coaches handled him so well, and the parents were so very helpful. Not only was hockey a great experience for Gabriel but for us as well.

Following the end of hockey, we registered Gabriel for swimming lessons where he really excelled. During the summer months he was in tykes' grassroots soccer playing with some of the kids from his hockey team.

We purchased and erected a trampoline and placed it close to his playset and swing. He loves "working out" on the trampoline and particularly enjoys it when friends join him. His enjoyment is focused on High River and Okotoks playgrounds, where he can spend many hours and always seems to make one or two acquaintances. It makes us feel great when we see his happiness and real enjoyment of people and things. He is now the focus of our lives and we treasure every minute we spend with him. Yes he requires work, but he keeps us young and happy, and the work is rewarding.

We also took two RV "camping" trips with him; one to North Spokane and one month later to Coeur d'Alene. He quickly made friends, was invited to a birthday party, and was even asked to accompany another family to Chuck E. Cheese. He rode his bike to visit his "friends" on specific camp roads and always checked with their parents to contact us to make sure he was welcome and not interfering. Our Gabriel was coming back!

As we continued to meet with Dr. Mendelson and she continued her sessions with Gabriel, she offered that she has seen a marvelous transformation in Gabriel. Over the six-month period that she has been seeing Gabriel, he has gone from "flat" to a real little boy. He has personality and can share feelings. He knows what he likes and doesn't like, and that goes for people as well. Dr. Mendelson continued to work with us until the episode of Jackson's refusal to allow us to continue therapy for Gabriel. When therapy is resumed, and it will be as it is very necessary and is showing results, we hope she will identify what the evil is that he hides from everyone.

Reflecting on the past two years the sheer stupidity of what has happened is mind-boggling. Two years ago, we were raising a beautiful, healthy, compassionate, and loving little boy. Two years ago, we were having issues of drug abuse and anger management with my son Jackson, but we maintained a "working" relationship. Then CFSA got involved. We lost our grandson and my son lost his son only to be given to unfit foster parents chosen as the "ideal family" by CFSA. After tearing our family apart through unsubstantiated accusations, causing horrific abuse and trauma to our grandson, causing untold damage, most of it irreparable, to our health, and subjecting us to out-of-pocket costs exceeding $133,000, and incidental costs approximating $6,600, our grandson is now returned to us. What has changed? Nothing, except that we now need to repair all the damage caused by CFSA. Our grandson needs psychological help, Jackson's finances have been severely depleted, and he now has a criminal record (real or fake, we don't know). We have untold expenses that severely cut into our retirement funds, and we can't undo the harm to our health. And they advertise themselves as Child and Family Services Alberta? How many other children and families must suffer these abuses before something is done to remedy this stupidity and evil?

CHAPTER 5

Fixing the System

Many years ago, while working in Edmonton, my husband had a boss that he truly admired and respected. He was president of the organization, had come to Canada from Hungary, and brought with him some "old" Hungarian sayings or proverbs. My husband's favorite, literally translated is, "the fish is smelling from the head." In plain old English, applying this saying to an organization means that if the employees of an organization are unprofessional, unqualified, rotting, and corrupt then you must look at the "head" of the organization as the cause. This old Hungarian proverb sets the scene for this chapter.

From the limited amount of research I was able to conduct in preparing to write this book, I learned from virtually all media sources that the province of Alberta has undertaken almost no improvements to their child care system. Media reports and two university studies credit the province of Alberta as the worst or second worst province in Canada with respect to child care capabilities, services provided, results obtained, and records maintained. Virtually nothing has improved since the days of the residential school fiasco, but each successive responsible minister has expounded on "improvements" made during his or her tenure. Ironically, the improvements were not for the vulnerable children and families but rather for the government. More power was granted to bureaucrats so that they could apprehend children and take them away from family to place them in foster care simply based on their opinions. Then, to protect these bureaucrats from potential prosecution, a publication ban was written into law thereby blocking any chance of family members from using the media to expose these illegal/immoral acts. So the claims by Manmeet Bhullar, David Hancock, and Heather Klimchuk that the protection of children and their families was paramount were nothing more than political fodder designed to make the electorate believe they actually cared.

Since any real change did not occur even after stinging media coverage, I feel that I must use the events and experience that my grandson Gabriel and our family endured to provide my observations and recommendations in the hope that sufficient public outcry can force some meaningful change. Also, since the new minister of Human Services is from a different political party and should not have any allegiances to any of the previous government's "smoke and mirrors" improvements, the time for meaningful change may be NOW! Allowing for some repetition of my research, in the next few paragraphs you will learn of my disappointments and then read about my approach at fixing the department. Uncaring, unprofessional, but most times mean-spirited people caused virtually all of our problems exacerbated by a poorly thought out Child Youth and Family Enhancement Act which actually promotes unsubstantiated, self-serving testimony from bureaucrats and their staff. Therefore, two things will need to be changed: people and the CYFE Act.

You must remember that our grandson suffered horrific abuse and trauma at the hands of CFSA. My son Jackson credits CFSA with the fabrication of information which resulted in a criminal charge (and this "criminal" information has yet to be disclosed by CFSA, possibly another fabrication) and the loss of his Okotoks residence costing him in excess of $80,000. And CFSA have negatively and severely impacted my health and my husband's health, most which up to this point is irreversible, and cost us more than $133,000 in out-of-pocket costs plus incidental costs approximating $6,600. So, I will be hard-pressed to be totally objective in my comments.

During the tenures of David Hancock, Manmeet Bhullar, and Heather Klimchuk as ministers of Human Services, the media severely chastised their department of Child and Family Services for the inferior quality of care provided to both children and families in their care. As the media seeks sensationalism, they concentrated on child deaths while in CFSA care. However, their second hot button was the Alberta government's publication ban on any children or families receiving care. They reasoned that such a ban was unconstitutional, did not protect children or families receiving care, but rather served only to protect the government from potential prosecution. In November 2013, David Hancock, then minister, was quoted as saying, "*yes there are tragedies* because we are dealing with a very difficult and tragic population, but we also need to say, *there's hope*" (emphasis added). He then reiterated his plan to form a roundtable with stakeholders and committed to reviewing Alberta child deaths and the publication ban. Then Manmeet Bhullar committed to the same reviews. However, during his tenure a four-year study undertaken jointly by the *Calgary Herald* and the *Edmonton Journal* released information that they found 145 foster children died between 1999 and 2013 while in care. This forced the minister to respond but his focus was on better accounting of the numbers <u>and somehow the reasons for the deaths got lost</u>.

The media storm resulted in further disclosures of child deaths while in care. A report by Karen Kleiss of the *Edmonton Journal* dated January 23, 2014 established that child deaths while in care actually reached 476. Yes, the accounting had improved but the "stop the bleeding" scenario had not been developed. Then came Heather Klimchuk who effectively passed the responsibility on to her department. So, we now have better accounting but still have not identified reasons and little improvement if any has occurred, yet the publication ban persists.

Looking into the negative impact on families caused by the Child Youth and Family Enhancement Act, I came across a very worthwhile website, pa-pa.ca/alberta.html. The research carried out by this organization clearly indicates that little if any improvement has taken place in Alberta dating back to the residential school fiascos of the early 1900s. In spite of that, great steps have been made by the Alberta government in "self-protection." The CYFE Act now empowers bureaucrats to remove children from their parents based on their opinions; and that's exactly what we ran into!

The feature article by Paula Simons of the *Edmonton Journal* on December 16, 2016 provides further proof of the criminal, immoral, and destructive antics of CFSA. Four-year-old "Serenity" suffered horrific treatment while in care and died in September 2016, but nothing had been reported to the RCMP for almost two years. However, the "statutory" director of Children's Services Eldon Block said his department did an internal review, but it was never forwarded to the RCMP. RCMP actually contacted the minister's department to ask for the information after they read the news stories about Del Graff's (Child and Youth Advocate) report into Serenity's death.

Tim Richter, chair of the review panel, was quoted "there's a real hard-wired defensiveness within the department…they're always under such scrutiny that their first instinct is to keep things quiet and keep their minister looking good." This ministry is in such a state of disrepair, caused in my opinion by unqualified, self-serving, and dishonest staff that another 71 children have died while in care in the province from 2014 to 2015. One cover-up seems to lead to another cover-up; people are just covering their respective behinds! There does not appear to be any appetite to clean up this quagmire, or are the people responsible too overwhelmed to be able to act appropriately?

In our particular case, proof of wrongdoing is so very extensive. Here are some specific points that identify either complete incompetence or systemic wrongdoing:

- Bonita Hoffman-Russell identifies that Janet and Jackson are not fit parents and must undertake significant rehabilitation before they have any real chance of regaining custody of their son. She also identifies that we (my husband and I) were very competently and effectively raising Gabriel. But instead of petitioning the court to continue my guardianship she switches allegiances, petitions for a Permanent Guardianship Order in favor of the director potentially removing our grandson from his family and making him available for adoption. Was there a master plan created between CFSA and the foster family? From this point onward every effort was made by CFSA to "give" our grandson to the foster family; no police checks, no safety proofing, no home inspections, no neighborhood checking, no requirements whatsoever from the "chosen" foster family.

- CFSA policies state that every effort should be made to keep the child within the family unit. However, in our case every effort was made to rip our grandson from our family.
- Management staff joined in supporting ill-conceived plans by caseworkers. Once they decided a course it was "win at all cost" and let's steamroll any opposition. No wonder CFSA child deaths while in care continue. Poor remedies which do not receive audit continue onward to become disasters. It has been proven that once a plan is put in place there is no room for deviation. That means that even if no risk assessments have been carried out the plan will proceed.
- CFSA staff proved without exception that they are incompetent, unprofessional, uncaring, committed to one solution; and heaven forbid if you should challenge them. They make your case their personal vendetta.

So, let me try my observations and recommendations on you. First, I believe that poor managers normally hire poor employees. Carrying that a little further and using actual case information, we have Associate Director Christina Tortorelli; she never responded to any of our letters or emails. Twice we reminded her that our email of October 7, 2014 was unanswered, and she completely ignored our important follow-up email of October 21, 2014. So, what is she doing there? She surely isn't working or just doesn't care!

Then we have Beverly Fournier, associate director and Pat Gilbert, manager. They reviewed and rejected our request for administrative review by simply "speaking" to Don Wijesooriya, manager, and John Hoveland, team leader, but did nothing else;

they did not investigate. They simply confirmed the decision of the perpetrators; who knows, maybe there was collusion? They therefore forced our grandson to further endure abuse and trauma caused by their completely unsatisfactory performance. If they are supposed to be protecting children in care, yet they are doing exactly the opposite and being paid, they must be replaced. Reviewing the decision of a suspect manager has responsibility especially when most people identify that manager as "difficult" and "not trustworthy," then due diligence is required … <u>not</u> simple concurrence. Besides, their statement of facts was also incorrect! CFSA does not need people like them.

Everyone to whom the October 7, 2014 email was addressed is next on my list:

- Linda Eirikson, manager, did not respond to our email and also completely ignored our second and third attempts at generating a response. What purpose does she serve in that organization?
- Don Wijesooriya, manager, refused to communicate in writing and refused to respond. He is in my opinion, together with Bonita Hoffman-Russell, the most dishonest, manipulative, self-serving person in the organization. He deserves special attention during my "fixing the organization" stage.
- John Hoveland, team leader, was given a copy of the October 7 email for his review and response. He unfortunately lied about responding and was caught in his lie by both Melani and my husband. Dishonesty has no place when dealing with the lives of children. He needs to be tuned up!

Now we concentrate on the worst offender to our grandson, Bonita Hoffman-Russell, caseworker. This person conspired with the foster family (the Fosters) to virtually kidnap our grandson without our knowledge and purposefully behind our backs. Other than Jackson's "bull-in-the-china-shop" explosions there was never any violence. Then CFSA got involved. We lost our grandson and my son lost his son only to be given to unfit foster parents as chosen by CFSA as the "ideal family." Then, CFSA, with the help of the Fosters, succeeded in demonizing Jackson through unsubstantiated and possibly fabricated CFSA accusations, so that he lost his Okotoks residence, was branded with a criminal record, and almost totally lost his son. Jackson claims that CFSA actions cost him roughly $80,000. Bonita Hoffman-Russell has proven to us that she is not only an unprofessional worker but also has proven to us many times over that she is a conniving individual that cannot be trusted. Evidence her claims and promises itemized that follow: 1) she said we could see Gabriel whenever we wanted after Gabriel's apprehension which she herself blocked (an outright lie!), 2) that she was working for us yet she pursued a PGO against us, 3) her initial affidavit contained so many self-serving errors that she promised to correct but never did, 4) that we were in mortal danger from Jackson, the reasons which have never been documented or proven, 5) that she arranged for Gabriel's apprehension in collusion with the Fosters without our knowledge and became angry and hostile when we found out, 6) that she was acting in Gabriel's best interest yet removed him from family protected by an EPO to place him in potentially dangerous foster care, 7) she deliberately demonized Jackson (without real evidence) resulting in his loss of residence and giving him a criminal record, 8) she wrote accolades on our parenting and then denied us visitation with Gabriel appointing instead the Foster family, 9) her most used phrase was, "Children are resilient; he'll get over it" (but why subject them to such trauma in the first place?), and the list goes on and on. What makes her so dangerous is because she has just enough believability to escape scrutiny, but has proven time after time to us that she lacks any moral fiber and definitely has no compassion for children and families and fabricates information to support her position. She was able to look both of us directly in the eye and lie to us without blinking and without shame. There is no place for such a person, especially when dealing with children and their families. However, she is supported by her supervisor Shauna Asselstine. Shauna rudely told me that RCMP law doesn't apply to CFSA and hung up on me. No room for discussion, no agreement to meet, nothing, just arrogance and ignorance. Again, there is no place for someone like her in a well-functioning organization.

Two other parties to this travesty are Margaret Bodeux-Tang, CYFE appointed counsel for Gabriel and lastly the foster family. Let's first look at Bodeux-Tang. She would be an embarrassment to the Law Society of Alberta (if the Law Society did its job) and most certainly to the director of CYFE, if the director position was in fact credible. Although she was appointed to represent our grandson Gabriel, as far as we know, she never met with him. She made emphatic negative comments to the judge about me without really interviewing me and completely ignored my husband. She made up the "facts" in order to hurt me but she really hurt her client. Her failure to adequately do her job not only caused my grandson to suffer more trauma and abuse, but also forced him to remain in a horrific scenario much longer than even CFSA felt was necessary. In my opinion she is potentially very dangerous to children and their families who may see her as their support, much as we had hoped and prayed.

Finally, we get to the co-conspirators, the Foster family or specifically Mr. and Mrs. Foster. Mrs. Foster strategically planned a child abduction, targeted at our grandson, and reeled in Bonita Hoffman-Russell as her accomplice. She completely fooled us until August 8, 2014, when she betrayed our grandson causing him unbelievable pain, abuse, and trauma. She betrayed Jackson twice and continued her betrayal of me and my husband until Judge Lipton put an end to it October 28, 2015. How can someone like her ever be given approval by government to operate a day home or provide foster care? She simply cannot fool everyone; which means no one checked out the Fosters before claiming that they were the ideal family. If CFSA is so high on themselves why is it that it took them one and a half years longer than it took for us to identify the Foster family fraud? It is this very practice of not checking foster homes or, in many cases, the specific family or families being considered to receive the child that contributes to the ongoing reports of child deaths while in care. If we know that there are deaths in custody, what other kinds of abuse are happening both physical and psychological?

Now that I have identified the perpetrators, we arrive at judgement day. I attempt to place the required corrective measures from least severe to most severe:

John Hoveland: Since both my husband and I consider John somewhat incompetent, over his head, and not interested in making any waves that might put him under scrutiny, his value today is minimal. He needs a stiff reprimand, told to shape up, and provided with clearly defined performance criteria. This is his ONLY second chance!

Christina Tortorelli, Shauna Asselstine, Beverly Fournier, Pat Gilbert, and Linda Eirikson: All are management representatives, and all shirked any responsibility whatsoever for providing any corrective actions which could have reduced the trauma to our grandson. They chose instead to bury their heads and let the chips fall wherever. They refused to provide any leadership although they have responsibility for leadership and staff development. Therefore there is no room for these people within the organization. Each should have their employment immediately terminated for cause and be released without any severance. Also, each requires a notation on file that they are not re-employable anywhere within government, especially as relates to children and families. Management has responsibilities but each has ignored their responsibilities and must suffer the consequences.

Bonita Hoffman-Russell: Bonita has proven to be one of the most devious people that I have ever encountered. She works to her own agenda all the while making you believe she is working with you. Anyone that uses government protection to secretly "abduct" a child from a guardian is pure evil. She therefore requires special attention. First she must be immediately terminated from her position for cause and certainly without any severance. Notations must be made to her file that she must never be reemployed by government or any crown board or agency of the government. Then, an independent body, preferably the RCMP or Calgary Police Service, needs to investigate her as I feel sure she has committed criminal acts especially in our case.

Don Wijesooriya: Now we reach the most destructive and dangerous person to children, families, and to CFSA that we encountered. Don obstructed any potential progress on our case every time he got involved. He outright lied to us, clearly made us aware that he would support the foster family against us each and every time notwithstanding the issue. He helped Bonita fabricate evidence to protect her instead of investigating our concerns. He attempted to block any attempt at communication. He refused to provide anything in writing other than notice of scheduled meetings. He broke CFSA policies simply to win. This man is potentially very dangerous and even more so because he is a management-level employee who affects the lives of many children and families. Therefore he must be immediately terminated from employment for cause without any severance whatsoever. His file must contain comments of his abuse and notes that he must not be reemployed by government or any crown board or agency of the government. Most importantly he must be investigated by the RCMP or Calgary Police Service for potential criminal activities. His actions along with those of Bonita Hoffman-Russell have resulted in so much child abuse, and when given the opportunity to correct the situation chose instead to do whatever was in their best interest not their client. They went out of their way to obstruct justice. They must pay the price for their criminal or at least immoral behavior.

Margaret Bodeux-Tang: Although she is not an employee of CFSA, she had a glorious opportunity to expose the criminal antics of CFSA regarding our grandson, and end the abuse and trauma to our grandson, but chose instead to fabricate stories to support the CFSA position. As she was an appointee of CYFE, it is imperative that CYFE learn of Bodeux-Tang's lack of performance, and most importantly, lack of real representation on behalf of her client, my grandson. Without any investigation she chose to demonize me and my husband and to support "babysitters" against us. She must not have read any of the affidavits written by CFSA attesting to our quality guardianship and parentship of our grandson. By her actions, she subjected Gabriel to an extended stay in sometimes dangerous foster care. Given that her only concern appears to have been her fees, not the appropriate care of her client, she therefore breaks her contract with CYFE. She must be removed as a resource for CYFE. She must be reported to the Law Society of Alberta where she should be reprimanded for behavior unbecoming of a member. She also needs to send me a written apology for her rude remarks and for the additional harm she put my grandson through.

The Fosters: This is a very sad story. There was a great opportunity to work together as "extended" family that could have benefitted both the Foster family and our Gabriel, but it was not to happen. Although we are both disappointed and angry with the Fosters' betrayal, we asked Gabriel how he feels in order to help us with our future dealings with or without the Foster family. When asked about the Fosters, Gabriel refuses to use their name. He simply refers to them as "the other house," crosses the first finger of each hand to form an X, and places it over his mouth. He now occasionally blurts out for what seems like no reason, "the other house are bad people." Some of his recent comments to us and to Dr. Mendelson indicate psychological abuse for sure, but he may also have suffered physical abuse. We may never know the full truth, but trust that Dr. Mendelson can shed some light on his issues in due course. If the Fosters wish to continue with any activity involving children such as day home, day care, or foster care, they must be ordered to undergo the appropriate training and certification. Because they have children who need a mother and father, we do not wish them any harm. A simple recognition that they caused severe trauma to Gabriel would suffice along with the return of his treasured Fisher Price toys and his convertible bed.

Now that we have cleared the slate of CFSA unqualified and/ or destructive staff, we need to overhaul some of the systems. First is the CYFE Act. This act gives so much power to the position of director of Child and Family Services that it becomes omnipotent. Remember the saying "power corrupts and absolute power corrupts absolutely"? Well the CYFE Act has actually recreated that very situation. No one, especially in government, should ever have absolute power. That causes the Shauna Asselstine scenario where RCMP law doesn't apply and we can do whatever we want. The act needs amendments placing parameters on the authority of the director's position and appropriate legal parameters for carrying out responsibilities under the act. And who or what is the director of Child and Family Services? There is never any name attached to that position. In our specific case the director is a bogeyman. In the director's name all kinds of unsubstantiated "facts" (or lies and fabrications) were presented in court as true without giving us the chance to challenge these lies. The director of Child and Family Services is nothing more than a figurehead, appointed by the minister by which CFSA can say or do anything, no matter how immoral or illegal and be free of prosecution. Unfortunately, and since the act is a very recent edition, incorporating meaningful changes may take some time. The section 120 (2) under which challenges may be undertaken against the director must be amended to become much fairer and to allow cases such as ours. Also any reference to a publication ban must be removed. This is unconstitutional in my opinion and serves only to protect the guilty. This is not at all included to protect children in care; rather it is clearly to frustrate anyone wishing to challenge the system. It smacks of a government that knows it is corrupt and needs every gimmick or impediment to frustrate any investigation or challenge. The publication ban MUST be removed.

Since the new minister comes from a different political party there are no allegiances to respect so we anticipated that the timing could be ripe for a top-down approach to implement much needed improvements. However, the new minister of Human Services Irfan Sabir's response to our inquiry was that he is very busy and that we should contact his associate director, Christina Tortorelli...the very same person that continually ignored us prior to him assuming his position. So, nothing changes; the administration just continues to grow, continues with their destructive ways, is not monitored in any manner, and re-creates itself and stays in a self-preservation mode. As in the past, the new minister can't be bothered. Once again, this minister mimics the same actions of all his predecessors, completely ignoring virtually "criminal" actions by his department, and requiring the perpetrators to audit themselves. How much more stupidly can so-called responsible elected officials think and act? Oh yes, in his letter to us he states, "As Gabriel has legal representation in all court matters, rest assured that the court process will ensure important decisions regarding his care are made objectively and in his best interest." He has not spent even 20 seconds investigating or he would have known that the apprehension was unlawful, that Bodeau-Tang's representation of our grandson was plain lies and complete fabrications, that family meetings were disbanded, that his associate director never responded to any of our requests, etc., etc. Must you have the lowest IQ possible to be Alberta's minister of Human Services? Wow! Just another form letter from that ministry but with several word changes! What a transition from an apparently uncaring and incompetent Heather Klimchuk to this...can it get any worse? To support the previous two sentences I provide a "sanitized" copy of Heather Klimchuk's response letter as well as Irfan Sabir's response letter in the supporting documentation section of this book. It is strange how similar these two letters are. And both ministers intimate that "they" (CFSA and the legal system) are more capable of providing the love, care, and necessities of life to Gabriel than are we. Is it any wonder that there is so very little trust in our legal system, CFSA, the judiciary, and politicians?

While reviewing media articles, I learned that Alberta is considered to be one of the three worst provinces in Canada providing child and family services. Articles also place Alberta as the worst or second worst province when Aboriginal families are included in the numbers.

So, I take a responsible position with this book because without looking for cases such as ours, 11 have surfaced just while discussing our case with friends and acquaintances. Eight have been brought to our attention by lawyers, technical writers, and support workers, and unfortunately these cases seem to very closely resemble ours. In all cases an apprehension occurred against family members in favor of foster homes. How can that be? Two more cases came to our attention while in High River at the water park. Again an apprehension took place against family in favor of foster homes. So, how can that be? In mid-August 2016 we received an email of another case in Claresholm; again, same type of case. Adding insult to injury, several of these families have been so terrified or traumatized by CFSA that they fear that even talking about their case will result in very severe retaliation by CFSA staff.

In our discussions, many versions of potential reasons for this immoral and abusive practice emerge; but the most prevalent seems to be that the more apprehensions a unit gets, the more budget they receive. Hopefully this rationale is completely flawed but just in case it does happen, then a remedy is to go back to zero base budgets. As I see it, more apprehensions expose CFSA to potentially more risk because of more children in care. So why not reward caseworkers for finding, through significant research, testing, and unannounced visitations "more appropriate" family members (not the kinship program but blood relatives or immediate family) to become guardians and place responsibility where it belongs, with the family? This could also reduce CFSA budgets to link directly with real required care cases. The current "practice" of apprehending from families to place children in foster care, especially when not really warranted, must be costly for CFSA: legal fees, foster home payments, increased risk of injury or death while in care, providing drivers, etc. We seem to be caught in a NATO type of government department, "No Action, Talking Only." When will the head of the fish take charge and make the required changes? CFSA cannot be all things to all people. Concentrate on real danger situations for CFSA intervention and place the other cases in the hands of responsible family members. Please do not place children in foster homes that have not been thoroughly investigated and certified. Imagine how stupid Don Wijesooriya must feel after stating on so many occasions that he and his team had placed Gabriel with the ideal family and that we were too old to be Gabriel's guardians. But some people insist on saying and doing such stupid things.

To make the organization one to be proud of you must hire several quality leaders that are professional, qualified, and committed with a real compassion for children and families. Having fewer top-notch employees, rather than the huge numbers now in CFSA who are incompetent and not invested, is so much better than too many barely adequate or proven non-performers content just to be receiving a paycheck. This attitude must start at the top, and the current slate of employees identified earlier in this chapter, as well as the new minister have proven they cannot or will not do the job. They cannot be part of the rebuild or it will fail. However, the CYFE Act actually encourages the criminal, immoral, and unprofessional antics of staff, based on our experience, through the position of director of Child and Family Services. That position for over two years was used by lawyers, caseworkers, and child advocates to accost us, lie to us, fabricate evidence, along with every other conceivable win at all cost scenario, without ever considering the real needs of our grandson. The director position has proven to be an offence to any law-abiding person, especially if dealing with CFSA.

Although it is difficult for someone like me to gain access to many of CFSA administrative procedures or policies, the few that I did see during the more than two-year period of this case seem to be well thought through. I do have real concern with the "global" application of the director position in the CYFE Act, its omnipotent approach to the director position, and director responsibilities, the publication ban and the inference that the director virtually cannot be challenged. If this act were amended to be more realistic, more transparent, and that <u>in court cases only the director or higher level can participate</u>, <u>not any appointee</u>, much improvement would occur. In our case, if staff had adhered to CFSA policies the apprehension of our grandson would never have occurred. So, I do <u>not</u> take issue with the policy but rather with those carrying out the <u>offense</u> of policy <u>contravention</u>. Therefore, all levels of staff involved in this contravention of policy must have their employment terminated, especially those at the management levels.

Now one more director-imposed impediment for which there seems to be no apparent reason. To write this book as factually as possible we asked our lawyer to return to us all of the property we left with him during our second meeting with him. His answer was that he could not comply as he had a trust condition with the director of Child and Family Services. That comment made us very angry. First, our property is our property and refusal to return same is theft, especially as the return of our documents was a condition of leaving those documents with our lawyer in the first place. Second, this raises the issue of whether or not our lawyer was really working for us or was he in a conflict of interest. Third, why does he not want to return our documents? Is there some skulduggery he is attempting to hide? Now it becomes imperative that our "entire" file is given to us as we have reason to be suspicious. Can't we trust our own lawyer? What trust condition does he have with the director of Child and Family Services? Do the director's tentacles reach into our own files? Where does invasion of our affairs stop? At the very heart of the matter is this fact: we <u>loaned our property</u> to our lawyer on condition that he return it to us, <u>to not return it is theft</u>. No matter what the director did or said with reference to "his" (the director's) documents has no effect on "OUR" documents! Now our lawyer tells us to petition the director for the return of our documents. His insistence that we petition the director of Child and Family Services or the Commission for Freedom of Information and Protection of Privacy (FOIP) is an attempt to force us to do his work. He has our property and he must do whatever he needs to do to return it to us...period!

So, to start the process we have petitioned the Commission for Freedom of Information and Protection of Privacy for release of our entire file to us. Unfortunately, we have lost confidence

In any government or quasi-government organization and after more than five months with the only notification so far being confirmation that FOIP has opened a file which appears much larger than expected and cost of retrieval is expected to be around $750 with tentative completion by August 2017. (Note: in October we actually received over 2,200 pages about 95% of them were redacted and completely useless, so we are still without OUR documents.) Since our lawyer created this problem, isn't it correct or even pure logic to expect him to pay that billing? As an additional source we contacted the complaints department of the Law Society of Alberta to register our complaint. Since this unreasonable additional impediment is created by our own lawyer, is there now reason to question whether or not he was doing his "best" job for us. Further, with Jackson now throwing into question the wording of the final court order and giving the order unintended meanings, it appears our lawyer did not provide the appropriate wording or protection we very much needed. This is disheartening as we now must hire another lawyer to draft a properly worded court order simply to be able to have Gabriel resume his counselling sessions with Dr. Mendelson. To our lawyer's detriment he has known from day one that Jackson was and would potentially always be trouble, yet in our opinion (which also seems to be confirmed by the Society of Psychologists of Alberta by their decision to recommend that Dr. Mendelson not continue counselling Gabriel until the order is corrected to be more specific), he did not provide appropriate legal assistance.

Unfortunately, especially for the director and CFSA staff, blocking us from the return of our property now results in us using our memory to make our assumptions, evaluations, accusations, and recommendations. Due to the unwarranted interference from the director, the chips will fall wherever they fall. In support of our position, and to further illustrate the two-faced actions of the director, we provide in the appendices a letter written by our lawyer to the director agreeing to provide the director with notes and documentation originating from Melani Carefoot, our resource from Positive Choices Counselling. Why can the director have unlimited access to any and most of our information, yet prohibit us from obtaining our own property? This position is a vile piece of government protectionism and has no place in an Alberta democracy. It is anti-children, anti-families, anti-openness; it is complete oppression!

This level of detail I feel is very necessary as I hope this book will assist Del Graff, Child and Youth Advocate, in his reviews and assessments of CFSA. From media reports it appears that some facts are hidden from him. Therefore my assessments which have documented proof should be helpful in his reviews.

Since my husband has very relevant and very significant experience conducting and developing performance criteria, we spent considerable time trying to present the foregoing actions without too much bias, but unfortunately much bias still shows.

Yes, we had to hire another lawyer to rewrite the Supervision Order. And this lawyer was able to obtain the reason for the "trust" condition between our previous lawyer and the director of Child and Family Services. It appears that our previous lawyer could not decipher the hen scratchings made by Bonita Hoffman-Russell included as disclosure documents that we left with him, so he turned our property over to CFSA asking that the documents be typed so they could be more easily read. Upon returning these documents to our lawyer, the director of Child and Family Services then placed a trust condition with our lawyer. This is pure garbage! Since we had unbridled ownership of the original documents, which we left with our lawyer on condition that he return them to us, they still belong to us. The director cannot dream up laws or impose conditions simply to support his case or to avoid further questioning and should not be exempt from prosecution for stealing our property. He has blatantly stolen our property. What kind of circus is this government running where law doesn't apply to CFSA staff and now even to the director? Just as worrisome are the actions of our lawyer. We charged our lawyer with responsibility for the return of our property to which he agreed. And then he reneges citing a "trust" condition with the director, and informs us to do his dirty work of retrieving our property by filing an order through the courts at our expense and applying to FOIP. When does reason prevail? Does it take a brain surgeon to advise an immoral and corrupt director that our lawyer has an obligation to us to return our property and the director's supposed "trust" condition therefore does not apply? When will responsible people act like responsible people? Is there really any hope to make positive changes to such a screwed up ministry, especially since every effort seems to be made to protect corruption at all levels, from the director level all throughout the organization.

To remake this ministry into a working and professional service entity, where staff are unquestionably representing their clients, not their own personal interests, something probably akin to what the original concept intended, there must be a willingness to be transparent and honest. So far those qualities or characteristics do not appear anywhere within CFSA, starting with the director, his/her staff, nor from the new minister.

CONCLUSION

We have gone through so much turmoil over the last two years. But one of the most vulnerable in our society, our little angel, Gabriel has suffered untold abuse, isolation, trauma, and whatever else may never be known. Unbelievably all the abuse and trauma was caused and deliberately administered by a department of the Alberta government specifically created to provide assistance and protection to children and their families. Child and Family Services Alberta, CFSA, especially the South Calgary and High River offices have proven that they seemed to delight in torturing our grandson. As mentioned in the last chapter, we now understand that 11 other families have undergone much the same unprofessional, verging on criminal treatment, from many of the same staff as we were forced to endure. Some of these families are still in the litigation stage which is extremely costly and gut-wrenching, especially when there doesn't appear to be a light at the end of the tunnel. All we can say to these families is don't give up hope; if you really love your child fight with every tool you can get your hands on.

Our plight with CFSA started in May 2014 and until late September 2015 we never saw a way of rescuing our grandson. No matter what we tried, CFSA was too powerful, too corrupt, and much too vindictive. Melani Carefoot kept reassuring us that CFSA did not have grounds to keep our grandson in care. But as the vicious CFSA machine tears away every hope, exasperation tends to take over. Although we initially thought we had a decent lawyer, he really couldn't sway CFSA away from their purpose which was to completely remove Gabriel from our family, and apparently to break us financially. Do you believe in Divine intervention? Well we do now.

In August 2015 we had virtually given up all hope of rescuing Gabriel, although we continued to go through the motions of fighting CFSA and we continued with our daily prayers very often questioning God if He heard us. But in persisting we received a very beneficial report from the CFSA appointed psychologist Sally During. Then the Fosters broke ranks with Jackson and immediately advised CFSA that they could no longer allow visitations between Jackson and Gabriel. The CFSA "ideal family" was unravelling and CFSA no longer had their ace in the hole to use against us. This resulted in the CFSA lawyer contacting our lawyer to advise that they found no reason to not return Gabriel to our care. So, it appears the psychological report and the four reference letters from friends, who had seen us parent Gabriel, in addition to the fallout of the Fosters with CFSA, became insurmountable evidence in our favor. The change felt like lightning striking; in August only despair, in September real hope! Just prior to our turn of events in September we heard, through my husband's sister in Montreal, about a husband and wife Christian missionary team that had visited us a year earlier who had promised us that they would pray relentlessly for the return of our Gabriel. The missionary's call, from Australia, to my sister-in-law in Montreal in September was to find out if "the little one was coming home" as they felt God was in the process of delivering an answer to their prayers. Imagine the timing of that call! Relating that story opened up many other such stories of friends and family also praying for the safe return of Gabriel. The reference letter writers as well as church friends all joined the prayer chain. So ask us if we believe in prayer and Divine intervention. How could everything realign in our favor without some Divine intervention? Even though CFSA had now advised that they would support returning Gabriel to us there was much to be done.

In the chapter "Life with Gabriel" we mentioned some of the unknown demons that were invading Gabriel's life. Again, in what appeared to be an answer to prayer, Dr. Mendelson was permitted to counsel Gabriel. Although we understood that this would be a long process, the inane actions of my son Jackson opposing Dr. Mendelson's assistance will extend the process and vitally hurt his own son. We have confidence in Dr. Mendelson, and we will work with her until she successfully removes the demons from Gabriel's life. This is a critical process as Gabriel now has complete trust in me and my husband but is still wary of most people, including his own father as he calls him "not dependable."

Here is a worthy note which represents a breakthrough that occurred in late June 2016. Gabriel was invited to the birthday party of his classmate Noah. As he happily talked to Papa about the birthday card he and Papa made and the gift for Noah he said, "at the other house birthday parties are only for family and we were family…but they weren't nice, they were bad." Slowly we are learning that life for Gabriel with the "ideal family" was not good. Perhaps Dr. Mendelson will learn more from Gabriel once we get the court order approved and Gabriel returns for his sessions. Gabriel has regressed during the four-month period that he has been blocked from seeing Dr. Mendelson, so getting court approval to resume counselling for Gabriel is imperative. For Gabriel's sake we are committed to carrying on with Dr. Mendelson until she breaks through Gabriel's tight veil of fear.

A note from our scribblings: We are now at May 2016, a full two years since the start of the attack by the Alberta government on one three-year-old child and a couple of senior grandparents. And although we had developed contingency plans for the care of Gabriel in the event something happened to us, nothing was ever put in place because of the inane amount of time spent fighting CFSA. As of today I am 69 and my husband is now 75 and our little angel is five years old. Yes, we know that Gabriel loves every minute that he spends with his dad and somehow Jackson now seems to be striving to re-earn the right and privilege to be Gabriel's dad. He and his girlfriend have parted and Jackson is placing real value on his time with Gabriel. However, he is away from home so often for work and at times has difficulty managing money. And since Jackson is employed in oilfield services he can be away from home for long periods or transferred to some other location, so he is realizing that a co-parenting role with us would be most beneficial to him. If Gabriel were to be returned solely to Jackson there would be issues of abandonment with Gabriel, which would be caused by those periods of absences. Those abandonment issues would affect school, sports activities, visitations with friends, and the list goes on. If Jackson was Gabriel's sole parent he would face significant costs for clothing, day care, amusement, etc., and would be forced to decide whether or not he could afford to register Gabriel for sports activities. Hockey registration this year alone will run around $675, some new equipment, one or two tournaments and the cost is easily around $1,200–$1,500.

We recognize that Gabriel really likes the stability he has with us, and since we are both "retired" he gets 100% of our love and attention. We consider ourselves truly blessed to be parenting our little angel. But how much longer will we be here and capable of raising Gabriel?

Jackson is showing more and more interest in wanting to see and to be with Gabriel. He has even relented and has agreed to continue play therapy for Gabriel with Dr. Mendelson. He has accompanied us on two short vacations with Gabriel and although it was not perfection, everyone had a good time. However, Jackson is so demanding of Gabriel; he expects Gabriel to read his mind and to do exactly what he is thinking. This is demeaning to Gabriel and he often tells us, after his father leaves, that he feels useless. We then reassure him that his dad has to learn how to deal with a five-year-old boy, but Gabriel is the farthest thing from useless. So, if Jackson is committed to learning how to relate to Gabriel and to understand that Jackson, himself, is not perfect there may be incremental hope.

We need to really plan for the future right now. As such, we are in the process of bringing together family members to work out a safety net for Gabriel. Jackson, with help from younger family members, raising Gabriel is becoming a feasible but not perfect solution. Some work still needs to be done as Jackson's work demands much of his time. Therefore, parenting Gabriel on his own, without a devoted partner, is an almost insurmountable task. Other than that, there are few real options within my immediate family. My husband does have two boys but neither has indicated any willingness to commit the time and resources that would be required to provide a loving environment to Gabriel. So nothing concrete has been developed to date. In the meantime, meetings are being planned with many other family members, as well as with completely committed friends who may become interested in doing what is best for Gabriel in the event something happens to me or my husband or both of us. Gabriel must never be put in the position of suffering such horrific abuse again.

Gabriel has a way of touching the heart of everyone that he meets. Even with all the trauma he has suffered, he has again become blessed with compassion and love, but he continues to be in pain and is searching for something, and for now nobody knows how to help him. He is truly our wonderful little angel.

May God bless Gabriel now and forever!

CORROBORATING EVIDENCE

AND DOCUMENTATION

Appendix A

The following inserts provide further proof of immoral and possibly criminal activities by CFSA. Most inserts are copies of emails, letters, or excerpts from personal and/or court documents. However all documents have been "sanitized" to remove names or information that is prohibited by Alberta law. Names of the perpetrators remain.

Email of October 21, 2014 asking for a response to our email of October 7, 2014:

> Follow up to phone call October 21, 2014 People
> 10/23/14 at 11:08 AM
> **To** Jessica Smith john.hoveland.ca.wijesooriya linda.
> eirikson christina.tortereli.
>
> To all that attended our telephone call of October
> 21, 2014
>
> After our telephone conversation yesterday we have
> some questions and comments which we detail
> below. As you will see from the e-mail below which

was sent to Mr. Wijesooriya and Ms. Eirikson some time ago we have already asked some of these questions but have not received any satisfactory feedback.

Don, per your phone call today, we will now contact Melani Carefoot to determine if and when she is available to attend and assist us as our support person in meetings with CFSA and Kinship providers. We will inform you as soon as we can confirm dates and times.

Although we asked many times during the telephone call what the risks were in our home; we have not received an answer. We took all necessary steps to protect Gabriel. If you had concerns about us allowing Gabriel to have access with his parents it should have been part of your assessment to discuss these concerns with us. We could have given you all the necessary information and the events surrounding all visitation. We will attempt to get a letter from the sponsor who attended with Jackson on Christmas Day and acted as a safeguard in the event that there were any concerns. What areas of concern do you have that would require a parenting assessment to be completed on us?

If our age is a concern to CFSA, although this would be discriminatory, we have already indicated that we would hire a nanny to live in our home to assist with day to day child care.

We were planning for the future as any responsible parental figures would, in the event of unforeseen circumstances. Just as people nominate guardians for their children in the event that they cannot care for them we were looking to do much the same by allowing ████████████to care for Gabriel to assess if this was a suitable placement in the event that one was required. This was our choice, and in our humble opinion a chance to assess the parenting capability of ████████████, and in no way indicated that we were wanting to relinquish care of him.

You spoke of us being grandparents to Gabriel. Should the PGO, that you have applied for, be successful and Gabriel is then adopted you will have no influence on whether or not we are included in Gabriel's future life. This is a very concerning issue to us. ████████████ have broken all verbal agreements they committed to with us and now won't even tell us where they live. What makes you confident that they would encourage any post-PGO contact, which is certainly not in Gabriel's best interest.

You also spoke of your wish to work on having Gabriel reunited with one of his guardians. We would of course be very happy if Jackson and Janet are able to maintain their sobriety and parent Jackson. If they are not then we wish to continue as guardians. As you are speaking about reunification plans why is your application not one for a temporary guardianship order? A PGO application is indicating that CFSA believe that there is not a guardian who Gabriel can ever be returned to. This would be inaccurate given the information you shared with us today. Are your plans to amend your court application? Why was it stated that the application 'starts as a PGO and then is reassessed after all parties have been assessed'? This is a contradiction to the Act you are obligated to follow that states the least intrusive intervention must be considered first. The fact that 'it is ultimately the court's decision and they can grant a TGO" is not the intended purpose of a court application. Should you not be presenting the correct application to the judge, and not expect him to figure it out?

As everyone participating in the telephone call made it clear that Gabriel's best interests should be at the centre of all decisions being made we wonder if this is in fact true. We asked a number of times why Gabriel's doctor and school had been changed. Mr. Wijesooriya, you stated that it was in Gabriel's best interest to attend a school nearer his home and not to be sat in traffic. Clearly Mr.Wijesooriya you have not read the file as Gabriel's original school program, Montessori, was also in Okotoks and only a short drive from anywhere in the town; and directly across from the Okotoks RCMP detachment. There was then a comment made about convenience. Convenience for whom? We would still like a definitive answer as to why Gabriel's school program was changed and why we do not know where he goes to school. He had a family doctor in Black Diamond. Was this also changed for convenience?

When will a play therapist be identified who can work with Gabriel? Will we be involved in this process?

Was there any court application last week as Jessica had indicated, No one got back to us about it despite us asking. We trust that any court matters will be conveyed to us, and I as a guardian will be served with the appropriate court paperwork.

I would like to attend the PKIC appointment. When is it?

Copy of previous email of October 7, 2014 follows:

Dear Mr. Wijesooriya and Ms. Eirikson,

Although the Initial Custody Order was granted last week, and despite your application for a Permanent Guardianship Order, I understand that your agency has an obligation to still work with our family. We are very concerned that as of yet we have not felt as if your employees have given us any assistance at all, quite the contrary. We feel the need to make a few points clear to you and as you have denied allowing us to bring our chosen support person to a meeting with you then we will inform you of these points, & ask questions, by e mail. The judge commented last week that he was not sure that CFSA actually had grounds for the apprehension order. An EPO was in place to protect us. We did not feel threatened by Jackson or Janet, the relatives with whom Gabriel had been staying voiced concerns that they were fearful after a phone call with Jackson's father. Why were we not allowed to pick up Gabriel from their home and allow the EPO to protect us as it is designed to do? D is a guardian and would have taken the necessary steps to ensure, as we both have been doing since the EPO was granted, Gabriel's safety. In the affidavit it states that Gabriel was in the vehicle when Jackson assaulted D. This is untrue. Gabriel was at home with R. This incident occurred in May, hence the EPO. Why was this grounds for apprehension in August? The RCMP officer also questioned this but when we attempted to discuss this with Shawna Asselstine she commented that this law doesn't apply to CFSA and hung up, ending the conversation. This was not only highly unprofessional but added to our distress. Why weren't less intrusive measures discussed such as a custody agreement if CFSA really believed Gabriel to be in danger and needing to reside elsewhere? Although we still maintain that Gabriel was not in any danger. In the contact notes it clearly states on August 13/14 that the RCMP do not believe that Jackson is a risk. In fact on 7 August/14 Bonita Hoffman-Russel had informed ███████ that the file was to be closed. Nothing else occurred, there were no changes to this file other than one phone call that made ████████████ feel unsafe, even though the person making threats was many miles away. ████ ███████████did not have to continue to care for Gabriel and could have dealt with their feelings of fear quite apart from us.

Why after the apprehension were we not allowed any access to Gabriel? We had to wait for three weeks until we could see him. We felt extremely distressed so we can only imagine how Gabriel felt being placed in a foster home with no contact with the people who loved him and had been caring for him.

Although we have limited access to Gabriel now we have many concerns about his well being in the home of ████████████████. If your mandate is truly to ensure the children's needs are considered why has Gabriel had to change his pre-school program? His place has been paid for at Okotoks Montessori, he is still living in this community and he would have benefited greatly from the consistency. We have not been told where Gabriel is going to pre-school now and have no information on the program. We are requesting that he return to Montessori immediately. Why has his doctor been changed? He has a family doctor in Black Diamond. Has he had any medical appointments since being apprehended, as we have not been notified of any. We have been told by the case worker that we are no allowed to go and watch Gabriel in his community activities such as gymnastics. Why has this decision been made? Why is he being transported to his visits with us by an agency, having to meet different drivers every week. Not only is this an unnecessary cost to the the government, it is not in Gabriel's best interest when we are more than willing and able to pick him up at ████████. We are not a threat to them in any way and would have hoped that they would have seen the benefit of working with us in Gabriel's best interest. This does not appear to be the case. We would like this changed immediately and either have ████████ drive him to our home or we will collect him.

Although D's mental health is in question, in your eyes only, we would like to make it clear to you that she has never had any mental health issues in the past, the doctor at the South Calgary Health Campus assessed her as fit and well other than situational distress. R does admit to sending an e mail to ████ ████ that was a fabrication. He did this in an attempt to make them understand how devastated D was. D never took an overdose or spoke of suicide and R understands how this could be misconstrued. He obviously regrets using this method as a way of attempting to make ████████████ understand how devastated they both felt and would have been happy to discuss this with your staff but was not asked or given an opportunity to do so.

We are able to assess risk. Last Christmas Jackson and Janet were angry with us for, in their opinion, withholding Gabriel from them. Jackson had not used for a period of 5+ days, Janet was sober and Jackson's sponsor was with them. We made the reasoned decision to allow Gabriel to spend time with them. We are diligent in not allowing Gabriel access to his parents if they have been using drugs. We are both well aware of the signs of drug use, have attended Al-An-On, and are able to effectively protect Gabriel.

As we are both older we had been exploring options that may be able to assist us in parenting Gabriel if he was to stay with us long term. As this was looking more likely with his parents unable to maintain sobriety we had been in discussion with Mr. and Mrs. Foster about how they might be able to assist. We were being pro-active in our planning and we had mentioned this both to CFSA and Gabriel's lawyer. This was then assumed to mean that we could no longer care for him now. That is not the case. Please see the safety plan below.

As our lawyer has now finished working with us we have the disclosure package. It is very concerning on many fronts. Bonita Hoffman-Russell's handwriting is so illegible for the most part that it makes the contact notes almost impossible to read, even with a magnifying glass. Please review the file and let us know your thoughts. As your notes, Mr. Wijesoooriya, are typed are we to assume that this is actually how contact notes should be recorded? On 25 August there is an e mail sent to us from ██████████ telling us how well Gabriel is doing with examples, yet on the same day there is a contact note written from a phone call between the worker and ██████████ which is absolutely opposite. Please review and explain what this might mean. We will send you our e mail for the purpose of referencing. The filing appears to be completely out of date order making the whole disclosure package very difficult to read or make sense of.

As part of our desire to ensure Gabriel's safety we attended at Rowan House Emergency Women's Shelter and had a meeting to go over how we intended to protect our family. The worker told us that we had done everything possible apart from inform our neighbours. We did so upon our return home.

No services have been offered to us to alleviate the perceived risk factors. What services will you be offering? What will be their goals?

No safety mapping meeting has been arranged as per your social work model, Signs of Safety. When will this occur? We have many friends, family and professionals who are able to attest that Gabriel is not at risk and who would be willing and able to report any concerns to CFSA should any arise.

SAFETY PLAN

EPO is in place until January 2015

A full time live in nanny will be hired to assist in day to day care of Gabriel

All visitation with the parents will be supervised by either an agency or the Safe Visitation Program A list of family and friends will be provided to CFSA to show the support system that exists for us.

Appendix B

The following emails outline the steps we had to go through to be granted "approval" to use Melani Carefoot as a resource in our meetings with Child and Family Services Alberta. The main obstacle was Don Wijesooriya. You can see through these successive emails, lies, cover-ups, and then pretense at wanting to help; all designed to protect him, CFSA and the foster family.

Sent: Tuesday, October 14, 2014 2:57 PM
Subject: Administrative Review & Don W

Melani:

Just heard from Don Wijesooriya via telephone. He says admin review will not proceed as our requirement to have you represent us is contrary to a section of the act. He will write to us quoting that section. But he would be agreeable to you assisting us as long as you don't attend meetings!!!!!

Also, I mentioned to him that Gabriel did not want to return to ███████ when we had him yesterday and that he needed to review the file contents. He said "they" decided that ████████████████ are the ideal family for the long term. So, what can we do? Is there really anyway to fight them?

We are visiting friends so we will have our cell on Thanks Melani,

Mr & Mrs.

To: "don.wijesooriya. " <don.wijesooriya@ >
Sent: Tuesday, October 14, 2014 8:16 PM
Subject: Re: Your phone message

Don:

Once you send me an e mail stating why we cannot choose our own support person and confirming that you have filed our administrative review I would be happy to speak with you.

I look forward to your response along with a response to my last e mail sent to you and Ms. Eirikson. I have also asked the case worker and team leader to advise us if there is court today (Weds) but again, and as always, have heard nothing. Can you please follow up on all of the above immediately and get back to us before the end of the business day today. Sooner if there is a court matter scheduled.

----- Forwarded Message -----
From: Don Wijesooriya <Don.Wijesooriya>
To:
Sent: Wednesday, October 15, 2014 6:44 AM
Subject: RE: Re; Your phone message

Good Morning Mrs.

I spoke to R yesterday and advised him of the status of the administrative review that has been filed. I continue to look to speak to you directly in order to provide you with the same information as well as an explanation around CFS's direction around meeting with the support person you have identified. A regional direction was provided to all of the CFS offices about meeting with the individual that you identified and I am more than willing to speak to you directly to advise you of those details.

I will also obtain an update about court proceedings and will provide you with that information.

Thank you,

Don Wijesooriya Manager Human Services

From:
To: "don.wijesooriya" don.wijesooriya >
Cc: "melani.carefoot" <melani.carefoot@ >
Sent: Wednesday, October 15, 2014 12:01 PM
Subject: Re: Request for Admin Review

Don:

On Page 80 of the CYFEA Policy Manual it states:

The responsible manager must determine if the request for the administrative review meets the legislative criteria.

- If a request for an administrative review meets the criteria for review per s.117.1, the review must proceed.

- If a request for an administrative review is received and it fails to meet the criteria per s.117.1, the person who requested the review must be advised in writing of the reasons why the request will not proceed and what other dispute resolution mechanisms are available.

As such please provide in writing as above why our Administrative Review was not deemed to be appropriate. Ms. Carefoot will be sending an e mail to you also outlining further concerns about your refusal to allow her to support us as we have requested.

Mrs

After Don reviewed the details provided in the above email he then changed his tune and sent a letter through Jessica to us but he does NOT quote the section of the act that he tried to blame, but rather states that he had the authority as per section 1.4.1 to make the decision; caught in another fabrication??

From
To: "melani.carefoot." <melani.carefoot>
Sent: Monday, October 20, 2014 3:31 PM
Subject: Fw: Letter

Melani:

We forward this e-mail from Jessica. Since we can't copy and forward Don's letter, here are some quotes

- In accordance with sec 1.4.1 of the Enhancement Policy Manual, as the manager of High River CFS Office, I have the responsibility to review this request and to assess if it fits the criteria......... upon reviewing policy, it has been determined that this request does not meet the criteria and therefore cannot be forwarded......

- As the decision by CFS was based on a directive by our regional leadership team and not a decision as per the CYFE Act, the decision cannot proceed.

He must really be worried about something. Are there higher levels of "criminals" that we can access in this corrupt organization?

Mr. & Mrs.

On Wednesday, October 22, 2014 4:47 PM, Don Wijesooriya <Don.Wijesooriya> wrote:

Good afternoon Mrs.& Mr,

I attempted to contact you this afternoon to advise you of an update to the directive that had been provided from our Regional Leadership team and how it relates to your request to have Melanie participate in a meeting with CFS. I will attempt to contact you tomorrow morning to discuss this further as it has implications for the admin review that you had submitted. In the short term and while a process is being carried out within the region, we will be able to permit Ms. Carefoot to attend the meeting as a support to you. As Ms. Carefoot can now attend the meeting that we have been proposing, it directly speaks to the decision that you have requested be reviewed through the administrative review process. Since you would be able to have the support person that you have requested attend this meeting and a reversal of an original decision has occurred, I need to speak to you about your filed admin review.

I look forward to speaking to you about this further tomorrow morning.

Thank you,

On Thursday, October 23, 2014 9:37 AM, Don Wijesooriya <Don.Wijesooriya> wrote:

Good Morning Mrs. and Mr.,

I have been attempting to contact you over the phone this morning but continue to receive a busy tone. We experienced this the other day as well when we were calling to speak to you on Tuesday. I understand that you have had some issues with your internet and am not sure if it is also affecting your phone service. I will be stepping out of the office at 10 and will be in meetings through out the day. I will continue to attempt to call you but in the event that we don't speak I wanted to pass on the information to you.

As I had previously indicated, the current direction is that Melanie can attend our meeting as your support which is what you had been requesting in your admin review. As the initial decision to not allow her to be involved has now been reversed, moving forward with this admin review would not be required. However, I would need for you to officially advise in writing that you would be withdrawing your request for the admin review as a result of the new decision. You can send me an email and I can forward your wishes to our regional authority office.

Thank you,

Don Wijesooriya Manager
Child and Family Services Division Calgary Region

Please note that Don W now does not want the administrative review to go forward and is appealing to us to withdraw it; what is he afraid of?

Appendix C

The following email was written to CFSA caseworker Jessica Smith, her supervisor John Hoveland, and their manager Don Wijesooriya. It was necessitated when I met the pediatrician chosen by CFSA and Mrs Foster for my grandson Gabriel. The pediatrician referred several times to the premise that Gabriel was being reviewed for adoption by ██████████and almost always addressed and exchanged conversation with her. I was the guardian, not ██████████ but some skulduggery had obviously taken place before the meeting among CFSA,██████████ and the pediatrician as evidenced by this email. I was virtually ignored by all parties.

From:
To: Jessica Smith <jessica.n.smith>;
John Hoveland <john.hoveland>;
Don Wijesooriya <don.wijesooriya>
Cc: Melani Carefoot <melani.carefoot>
Sent: Wednesday, November 19, 2014 4:49 PM
Subject: Gabriel's doctor visit / Friday meeting

Good afternoon Jessica, John and Don

We are following up on the telephone conversation that Melani Carefoot had with Jessica on our behalf and the voice mail that she left for Don. As John's voice mail message stated that he was away from the office no message was left with him.

When Melani spoke with Jessica at 10 am this morning she asked her to call D to allay her concern that the case plan for Gabriel was in fact adoption. Jessica confirmed that she would call. (Don was asked to make contact with us in the voice mail). As it is now the end of the work day for CFSA employees we assume that this will not in fact occur. How can we build a collaborative working relationship with CFSA when they do not carry through on tasks that they have agreed to? This lack of trust also raises the question about the true case plan.

At the paediatrician's appointment yesterday the doctor mentioned adoption three separate times. Jessica assured Melani that this was because this doctor often completes pre-adoption medicals. We will be following up with the doctor ourselves to ensure that she had not been given the impression that ██████████ was being considered for adoption. The conversation certainly appeared to be conducted in such a way as to suggest that this is a conversation that had occurred prior to the appointment. The doctor had no idea that D was going to attend and D's input was minimal, with ██████████ information being the main focus.

No R & E has been submitted for play therapy as was agreed on at our last meeting on 5 November. We understand that Marlene Laberge-Oneill has a contract with CFSA and as she is a well-known attachment therapist (the paediatrician mentioned her yesterday) and she has an office in south Calgary we would like to request that she is contacted immediately to begin working with Gabriel and ourselves.

As Gabriel currently has a broken collar bone we would ask that he is given cows milk instead of soy milk as the calcium contact is far higher. We feel that this is important for his bone repair. We took Gabriel for a haircut whilst he was visiting with us today.

As requested in the previous e-mail we would still like to go ahead with the meeting scheduled for Friday 21 November/14 and could meet earlier (around 4pm). As the meeting was already scheduled we trust that this will be possible. If for some reason this will not work please let us know of your availability on Monday or Tuesday of next week. We would like to meet with you aside from the main group to express our concerns, some of which may be alleviated once the two e-mails that we sent weeks ago are responded to.

We look forward to hearing from you.

Fax

To: The Honourable Manmeet S Bhullar
   Minister of Human Services
Date: August 26, 2014

Fax No. ███████████

From:
Tel:

Message
I am reporting on a disastrous experience I have had with your High River office and specifically the abuse received from Bonita Hoffman Russell and her supervisor, Shauna Asselstine.

The attached (2) pages outline my case. Your office and specifically the Child, Youth and Family Enhancement Act are supposed to protect children and provide services which are in the best interest of children.

Through a conspiracy of lies and "imagined" dangers my grandson was taken from the "kinship" home in which I placed him without any consultation with me, his guardian, and placed in Foster care. What good are Court Orders appointing me his guardian as well as granting me parentship, if he can be traumatized by FCS, by taking him from loving families and placing him in Foster care.

Since he was in my care without incident for more than one year, he should have been returned to my care until FCS and the kinship parents ironed out their issues, not taken and placed in foster care. That was TOTALLY traumatic to my grandson. But even worse, I am the only blood relative in his life and FCS has prohibited me from any unsupervised contact. Two and one half weeks have passed and FCS still prohibits me from seeing my grandson.

Please investigate immediately.

Thank you

5/28/2019

From: ███████████████████████████
To: hs.minister@gov.ab.ca
Date: Thursday, August 28, 2014, 11:48 AM MDT

I am shocked that no one from your office has acted on this very very important issue. I guess "the groundbreaking" legislation to protect children and the family is just more crap for voters to swallow.\

Yesterday when we were granted 80 supervised minutes to visit with our grandson we questioned why our every movement was watched by incompetent, malicious caseworkers. Then we realized that our ██████ was not the exuberant, loving 3 1/2 year old that your workers abducted 3 weeks ago. He was distant, almost non-communicative, no laughing or smiling, no running; it was like he had been drugged. He needs immediate medical attention; but not from any of your unreliable caseworkers.

We need to immediately take him to a doctor as we fear that he is now suffering from detachment disorder. But that seems to be a common occurrence to most of your abducted children! Why are you so intent on damaging children instead of protecting them?

All you need to do is terminate the services of those malicious non-caring caseworkers and supervisor and formally return ██████ to us, where he has always had nurturing, care, safety, unconditional love, and of course been protected from abandonment until your heavy-handed workers broke all the rules.

If we do not immediately receive unrestricted access to ██████ and you interfere with us taking him to a doctor you will face legal action. Do the morally right thing now.

████████████████

PASCAL RONALD

From: ▮▮▮▮▮▮▮▮▮▮▮▮▮▮▮▮

To: ▮▮▮▮▮▮▮▮▮▮▮

Date: ▮▮▮▮▮▮▮▮▮▮▮▮

To: "hs.minister@gov.ab.ca" <hs.minister@gov.ab.ca>
Cc: "premier@gov.ab.ca" <premier@gov.ab.ca>; "ministryofjustice@gov.ab.ca"
<ministryofjustice@gov.ab.ca>; ▮▮▮▮▮▮▮▮▮▮▮▮▮ <▮▮▮▮▮▮▮▮▮▮▮
Sent: Thursday, September 4, 2014, 7:51:15 PM MDT
Subject: Justice for ▮▮▮▮

We have written to you by fax and then two follow-ups by e-mail but to date your office has not replied. We are very concerned re the completely unnecessary trauma caused to our grandson by your department of Child and Family services. We finally saw him under supervision by CFS and now know why we have been prevented from seeing him till now. He is not the same happy lovable child your department abducted from us. He is vacant, non communicative, fearful (even of us). What have you done to this beautiful 3 1/2 year old. It is really sad that the department charged with protecting children and the family has instead inflicted serious trauma to a 3 1\2 year old child and the grandparents that raised him. And you don't seem to care? Where are the resources to investigate what has to be malicious behaviour by some of your people. Are you not responsible for this department?

Yours Truly,

Name and Address

Telephone:

September 13, 2014

The Honourable Manmeet Bhullar,
Minister of Human Services
Alberta Legislature

Re: Gabriel and Child and Family Services High River Office

Dear Mr. Minister:

I sent you some e-mails regarding this topic while I was very angry because of the trauma being caused to my grandson by CFS High River office. Now that my anger has subsided, but my disillusionment and complete disappointment remain, I need to make you aware of performance, integrity, moral and trust issues with at least two staff members of the CFS High River office, Bonita Hoffman-Russell caseworker and Shauna Asselstine (sp?) her supervisor. As I realize CFS has an important role in Alberta society, I am worried that if other Albertans are betrayed such as I have been, you will face many law suits and potential violence.

Here are the facts in chronological order:
1) ▆▆▆ (my grandson) was placed in CFS care because his biological mother was abusing drugs and the court awarded me guardianship.
2) After ▆▆▆'s biological father (Jackson, my son) failed to appear in court due to also using drugs I was awarded both guardianship and parentship.
3) We (my husband and I) met with Bonita who advised that we were doing an "awesome" job of raising our grandson as he was happy, well-adjusted and very loving.
4) To further enhance Gabriel's lifestyle and also due to our age we investigated au pairs and nannies.
5) A distant cousin ▆▆▆ advised she and her family wanted to raise Gabriel, firstly in "kinship" then with a view to adoption.
6) We were ecstatic as ▆▆▆ had 3 children around Gabriel's age, so we cleared that proposal with Bonita.
7) After several months with everything going well, Bonita advised ▆▆▆ that she would close the file.
8) Bonita suggested to ▆▆▆ that she call Jackson (Gabriel's father) a hard core addict to discuss financial assistance, visitation, etc.
9) ▆▆▆'s call was intercepted by Trevor (Jackson's father) who made a comment that ▆▆▆ interpreted as a threat.
10) Instead of returning Gabriel to us, if she were indeed concerned about Gabriel's well-being, she phoned Bonita who immediately arranged for an apprehension, without even advising us.

11) Gabriel was placed in a foster home for almost 3 weeks. We were not allowed to know his location, or any contact, but surprisingly the kinship family had continuing contact.

12) Gabriel had already suffered much trauma; losing his biological parents and home, losing his grandparents love and home, and now losing the kinship home. This could have been avoided if Gabriel had simply been returned to us.

13) Gabriel was returned to the kinship home but Bonita continued to forbid us any contact.

14) After court on August 18, 2014 after repeated attempts to see Gabriel, Bonita finally consented to "supervised" access. On just 2 visits totalling 2 ¼ hours we then realized the horrific trauma Gabriel has suffered. From a happy, well-adjusted, loving child, CFS has turned him into a vacant, unhappy, scared little boy. This makes us very angry because it was completely unnecessary. And it caused very much damage to Gabriel, from those entrusted with his well-being.

15) We repeatedly asked for more than one month, why we cannot see our grandson, unsupervised, but no answer.

16) Finally September 11, 2014 we were granted a meeting with Don (?) Manager who seemed to know there was something very wrong with our case but tried without any success to cover it up. But he did focus on statements by Bonita attempting to cast allusions of potential instability. I resent her personal attacks on me simply because I disagreed with the way she managed this case and the damage she caused to my grandson. However I now have the right to call her what she really is: a fabricator of lies to justify her end goals, an uncaring, heartless person who should never be allowed to destroy other children and families.

17) Yesterday Gabriel was brought to our home for a 2 1/2 hour supervised visit. When it was time to leave, he cried and hung on to us not wanting to leave. Can you not see the trauma and damage that CFS is causing?

18) On September 23, 2014 CFS will go to Family court to seek Permanent Guardianship for our grandson. Why would you allow that when we have always provided a safe, caring and loving home? Why not return him to our guardianship and parentship? This isn't about a political fight between us and CFS; it is about the appropriate caring for our grandson!

19) Under the "care" of CFS Gabriel has suffered much trauma, has suffered from discontinuing relationships, continuous exposure to one stranger after another, loss of trust, loss of loving grandparents, loss of people who really care. What we hear is; he is resilient, he'll get over this! Well why create the distress in the first place? There is NO valid reason, and we now know that! Therefore we respectfully request that instead of pursuing a PGO for CFS, CFS respectfully recognize our ability to care for Gabriel and support our continuing TGO and "parentship" order for our precious grandson.

The Gabriel that used to be a happy, loving, considerate little boy, has now become "broken" because of the intervention of CFS. He is a little boy who needs love and stability due to his loss of virtually everything in his life. ████ made a real issue of teaching Gabriel to not go to strangers in public areas, but now that's what he has daily, caseworkers, other social workers, visitation supervisors, their family members, their friends, new school, new teachers. Not one part of his life is / has been stable since CFS apprehension. The trauma, which is very evident, has been severe to the point of personality change. But those that the Alberta government appoints as protectors keep saying; "he'll get over it", "kids are resilient". Is it their intention to push these children to the limit to see if they will break? We wish, hope, and pray that there might be just "ONE" person that will do the right thing for our grandson. JUST ONE!

Although the concept of CFS is great, the delivery in our case is abysmal. In High River, caseworkers such as Bonita and her supervisor are not only unqualified and uncaring but also morally corrupt and should be immediately fired. And it is not necessary to continue the current cover-up. We now know the conspiracy that was committed, the errors, the lies. It is time to appoint an independent third party to properly investigate and to provide firm recommendations for improvement so that these errors whether intentional or not do not recur. And please, provide for us unsupervised access to Gabriel anytime we want. Nobody loves him and cares for him more than we do!

Sincerely,

Signed

PS:
Yesterdays CFS supervisor of visitation asked us why we were required to have supervised visitation. When we said we did not know, he answered that we have the most loving family of any that he has visited so far.

I also attach a copy of an excerpt from the CFS affidavit describing the quality of care we have provided to ▓▓▓ which again begs the question; what have we done wrong other than challenge Bonita's handling of our case?

(Note that the excerpt was never returned to us by our lawyer)

PASCAL RONALD

ALBERTA
HUMAN SERVICES
Office of the Minister

October 31, 2014

 and ▇▇▇▇▇▇▇

▇▇▇▇▇▇▇

Dear Mr. ▇▇▇ and Ms. ▇▇▇▇

The Honourable Jim Prentice, Premier of Alberta, forwarded your letter regarding concerns for your grandson, ▇▇▇ to me for further response. I am also in receipt of your correspondence to the former Minister of Human Services and to the Minister of Justice and Solicitor General. As Minister of Human Services, I appreciate the opportunity to respond.

Let me first apologize for the delay in addressing your concerns. I recognize your love for ▇▇▇ and your desire to see him in the best of care. The Ministry of Human Services is committed to the safety, protection and well-being of all children, and decisions regarding the placement of children are made with a focus on their best interests. As well, to minimize the potential trauma for children in care, every effort is made to help them maintain family connections.

I have shared your concerns with Calgary Region Child and Family Services (CFS), who indicate ▇▇▇ extended family has been permitted frequent contact with him and that he appears to be well settled and enjoying his kinship home.

I understand you met with Mr. Don Wijesooriya, Manager, Calgary Region CFS, to discuss ▇▇▇ care and the potential to move toward unsupervised visitation. I am pleased to hear you are now engaged in regular, unsupervised visits with ▇▇▇ and that you will be seeking a support person to attend a proposed family meeting with you. Options for ▇▇▇ long-term care will be discussed in a collaborative setting utilizing the Signs of Safety mapping process, an effective tool that will ensure any protection concerns pertaining to ▇▇▇ well-being are addressed.

...../2

Page 2

As ████ has legal representation in all court matters, his best interests will be considered in decisions regarding his care as legal matters proceed and are resolved through the court process. I encourage you to consult with legal counsel with any questions regarding court processes. You may wish to access the Law Society of Alberta's Lawyer Referral Service at 1-800-661-1095. Student Legal Assistance is also offered by the University of Calgary's Faculty of Law, who can be contacted at 403-220-6637.

Mr. Wijesooriya would be pleased to discuss these matters with you should you wish further clarification. He can be reached at 403-297-6427 or by email at don.wijesooriya@gov.ab.ca.

Thank you for writing and sharing your concerns.

Best regards,

Heather Klimchuk
Minister

cc: Honourable Jim Prentice
        Premier of Alberta

        Honourable Jonathan Denis
        Minister of Justice and Solicitor General

PASCAL RONALD

November 5, 2014

Honourable Heather Klimchuk,
Minister of Human Services,
224 Legislature Building,
10800 – 97 Avenue,
Edmonton, Alberta T5K 2B6

Re: Violation of 3 ½ year old grandson's rights and grandparent rights by High River
Office of Alberta Child and Family Services

Dear Minister Klimchuk:

We are appealing to you as our last resort for justice and fairness in our dealings with
CFSA High River office. A brief summary follows and we include several attachments
to give you some perspective on our case. Key details follow:

1) We (the), grandparents) have been full-time caregivers (was court appointed guardian
and had parenting responsibilities) to our grandson, Gabriel for almost 1.25 years, during
which time he was safe, secure, well cared for, well-adjusted and a happy very active
child.
2) In June 2014 a distant cousin with 3 children much the same age as ████ proposed
that she would like to eventually adopt Gabriel as he would perfectly fit their family and
he would then have siblings. We agreed to a trial "kinship" arrangement with the
concurrence of CFSA, mainly because Gabriel "loved" to be with children.
3) On August 8, 2014 without our knowledge the "kinship" family and CFSA
apprehended our grandson and placed him in a foster home. When we found out we
fought them, and tried to take Gabriel home with us, but CFSA said they had the
authority and just trampled our rights.
4) From that point onward we have been almost totally forbidden from access to our
grandson, even though he was returned to the"Kinship" home after approximately 2
weeks.
5) We have phoned, met with, sent e-mails to the caseworkers, supervisors, and manager
but they refuse to discuss anything with us.
6) Because of the subterfuge perpetrated by the High River Office we now believe they
have not only acted immorally and illegally, but have also contravened the Act and the
corresponding policies.

Three employees that have been instrumental in breaking CFSA policies, fabricating false
information and covering up department mistakes are, Bonita Hoffman-Russell,
caseworker, Shauna Asselstine, supervisor, and Don Wijesooriya, Manager.

We have spoken to many friends, family, and acquaintances who have all indicated that
they have heard many such stories and that we should write to you, the Minister of
Human Services for rectification, and to have our grandson returned to us.

Please, please review this case at your earliest convenience and return Gabriel to his rightful home, with us. We know he has suffered horrific trauma while in CFSA care as well as while in "Kinship" care. But the CFSA answer to our pleas has been "kids are resilient, he'll get over it" And this from people that are supposed to be protectors of children. Again we ask that you intervene before Gabriel's scars become so deep that there is no coming back!

Because we earnestly have Gabriel's best interests at heart we are prepared to come to Edmonton to meet with you at your earliest convenience, bring all documentation and to work to a mutually acceptable resolution with you.

Sincerely,

Encl: 2

November 14, 2014

Honourable Heather Klimchuk,
Minister of Human Services,
224 Legislature Building,
10800 – 97 Avenue,
Edmonton, AB T5K 2B6

Dear Minister Klimchuk:

We received today your reply to our letters and e-mails requesting your assistance with respect to the immoral, unethical and sometimes criminal treatment by Calgary Region Child and Family Services (High River office) to our grandson and to us. Since you have not investigated, but rather asked the "perpetrators" to audit themselves you will never get to the truth of our case. And it is impossible for us to "work with" Don Wijesooriya as he has been instrumental in covering up the subterfuge undertaken by his staff.

Because of relying on the word of "those" that have broken CFS policy, lied, created false documents, etc., to cover up their dishonest deeds you will never know the following:

1) Caseworker Bonita Hoffman-Russell initially disclosed in a court affidavit that we were excellent guardians as Gabriel was well-adjusted, happy, active, and a compassionate little boy.
2) Caseworker Bonita Hoffman –Russell, just two months later vilified the biological father by insisting to us that she had information that he was dangerous, our lives as well as our grandson's life were in danger, without ever providing supporting information.
3) Caseworker Bonita Hoffman-Russell on August 8, 2014 conspired with ████████ (Kinship home) to apprehend our grandson and place him in foster care without our knowledge or consent, and blocked us from collecting our grandson and bringing him home. (Contravenes CFS policy)
4) Caseworker Bonita Hoffman-Russell told us that CFS has a huge slate of lawyers and fighting CFS would break us.
5) Caseworker Bonita Hoffman-Russell insisted we could have access to our grandson any time by simply asking her, yet she blocked us from any contact for almost three weeks.
6) When we inquired with the RCMP Okotoks detachment, they advised us CFS acted illegally. We then spoke to CFS supervisor Shauna Asselstine who told us "their law doesn't apply to us" and hung up.
7) We called Don Wejisooriya for assistance to have our grandson returned to us but his comment was "he is with the ideal family". And he said that if we showed even the least bit of anxiety he would not meet with us. Wow! he believes he is an infallible god!
8) At Family Court, September 29, 2014 Judge ████████ summarized his review by saying that he wasn't convinced that CFS had justification in apprehending our grandson.

9) We have written two e-mails (attached) asking for our questions to be addressed by your entire CFS team, including Don Wijesooriya to which we have had no reply. E-mails are dated October 7 and 23, 2014.

10) Don Wijesooriya did everything in his power to block our use of Melani Carefoot as our resource. We had to resort to an administrative review to get her accepted. Why?

11) CFS continues to treat the Foster home as the **guardians** and refuses to tell us where our grandson is living, or why his school has been changed, or why his doctor has been changed or why they are waiting so very long to have him psychologically assessed Is CFS afraid of the findings?

12) Our grandson has not only suffered trauma while in CFS care but now has also suffered a cracked collar bone. Will this become another case to add to the more than 700 child deaths in CFS care?

You can tell from the few events illustrated above that your Calgary Region CFS team has broken your policies, acted deceitfully, if not criminally, and cannot be trusted to tell the truth. They are busy covering their tracks as they know we have caught them in their lies, deception, and criminal activities since we now have the disclosure documents. **Their main concern is to hide the truth and to keep their jobs; not to protect our grandson! We are the only ones who really love and protect our grandson but that has been illegally taken from us by CFS.**

Before any further damage is caused to our grandson, you must undo the evil and the damage caused by your CFS team and return our grandson to us where he is loved, safe, nurtured and a priority. **Then please conduct an independent third party review of our case, bringing to justice those that have a part (Bonita Hoffman-Russell, Shauna Asselstine, Don Wijesooriya, among others) in this unethical, immoral and criminal activity and cover-up.**

Yours sincerely.

cc: Honourable Jim Prentice, Premier of Alberta

cc: Honourable Jonathan Denis, Minister of Justice and Solicitor General

June 18, 2015

Honourable Irfan Sabir,
Minister of Human Services,
402 Legislature Building,
10800 – 97 Avenue,
Edmonton, AB T5K 2B6

Re: Complaint against Child and Family Services Calgary Region by

Dear Mr. Minister:

We enclose copies of our last letter, regarding the above noted topic, addressed to
Heather Klimchuk (cc Jim Prentice and Jonathan Denis) and attachments mentioned in
that letter. Unfortunately, none of the addressees bothered to investigate or even get back
to us, a typical trait of the previous out of touch government.

Due to your short time in the legislature and the horrendous amount of work you must be
facing at this time, and our respect for your office, we feel nervous about once again
bringing up the terrible, unprofessional, unethical and immoral treatment of our grandson
and us by CFS employees of the Calgary Region. Notwithstanding the foregoing, we are
so very concerned about the on-going harm and psychological abuse that our grandson
continues to suffer; such harm appears to be fully acceptable to CFS Calgary Region.
Even the "ideal foster family" deliberately chosen by CFS for our grandson to spite us
because we were strongly opposed, and continues to be completely protected by CFS is
now reneging on their role causing more trauma to our grandson, indicating we were
right in the first place!

It is our desire to meet with you or your Deputy and to bring with us all the appropriate
documentation so that you can have detailed proof of the unprofessional and unethical
actions of CFS Calgary Region staff. Hopefully you can then provide an avenue for a
"meeting of the minds" and we can resolve what now appears to be an angry stalemate.

Thank you for your attention to this matter.

Sincerely,

ALBERTA
HUMAN SERVICES

Office of the Minister

July 15, 2015

and

Dear Mr. and Ms. :

Thank you for your recent letter regarding the care of your grandson, . As Minister of Human Services, I appreciate the opportunity to respond.

The protection and well-being of children is a key priority of the Ministry of Human Services, and I expect all department employees to be professional, respectful and ethical in working with the people we serve. Feedback regarding poor client service is taken seriously.

Your correspondence has been shared with Calgary Region CFS and I am advised they are aware of your concerns for in his current kinship placement. It is my understanding that planning for s needs are addressed during family meetings. Calgary Region CFS will be pleased to discuss your concerns at the next meeting scheduled for August 7, 2015.

As has legal representation in all court matters, rest assured that the court process will ensure important decisions regarding his care are made objectively and in his best interest.

Unfortunately, my schedule does not permit me to accept your offer to meet at this time; however, I encourage you to contact Ms. Christina Tortorelli, Associate Director, at , should you wish to report or discuss any new issues before the next family meeting.

Thank you again for taking the time to write.

Sincerely,

Irfan Sabir
Minister

402 Legislature Building, 10800 - 97 Avenue, Edmonton, Alberta T5K 2B6 Canada   Telephone 780/415-4815 Fax 780/415-4319

AR 50580

145

Excerpt taken from CYFEA (Calgary Youth and Family Enhancement Act)

Please note Child Apprehension Policy

Chapter 5: CYFEA Agreements and Orders

Section:	**5.3 Orders**	Issue Date: October 1, 2011
Subsection:	**5.3.1 Apprehensions**	Revision Date: October 1, 2011
		Page 1 of 7

Policy

Apprehend a child **only** if:

- the child is in need of intervention per s.1(2),
- less intrusive measures cannot adequately protect the child, and
- remaining in the current situation will endanger the child's survival, security or development.

Approval from a supervisor **must** be obtained prior to making an application for an apprehension order or completing an emergency apprehension.

> NOTE: A peace officer may also complete an emergency apprehension under s.19(12) or (14).

Purpose

Apprehending a child is an intrusive measure, used when less intrusive measures will not adequately protect a child, that sets in motion a series of events requiring both legal and casework attention. As a result, consider:

- Under which section of 1(2) is the apprehension to be executed?
- Will forced entry be necessary?
- Is a treatment order needed?
- Are secure services needed?
- How will the apprehension be executed? (e.g. is police assistance required?)
- Is the child an Indian child and, if so, residing on reserve?
- What actions to take after the apprehension?
- Whether an application for an Emergency Protection Order under PAFVA could alleviate the need to apprehend in situations where there is domestic violence or severe domestic disharmony?

Enhancement Policy Manual -- Intervention

(t.1) "reserve" means reserve within the meaning of the *Indian Act* (Canada);

(u) "secure services certificate" means a secure services certificate issued under section 43.1;

(v) "secure services facility" means a facility designated by the Minister, by regulation, as a secure services facility;

(w) "secure services order" means a secure services order made under Part 1, Division 4;

(x) repealed 2003 c16 s3;

(x.1) repealed 2008 c31 s2;

(y) "supervision order" means a supervision order made under section 28 and includes a renewal order;

(z), (aa) repealed 2003 c16 s3;

(bb) "temporary guardianship order" means a temporary guardianship order made under section 31 and includes a renewal order;

(cc) "youth" means a child who is 16 years of age or older.

(2) For the purposes of this Act, a child is in need of intervention if there are reasonable and probable grounds to believe that the safety, security or development of the child is endangered because of any of the following:

(a) the child has been abandoned or lost;

(b) the guardian of the child is dead and the child has no other guardian;

(c) the child is neglected by the guardian;

(d) the child has been or there is substantial risk that the child will be physically injured or sexually abused by the guardian of the child;

(e) the guardian of the child is unable or unwilling to protect the child from physical injury or sexual abuse;

(f) the child has been emotionally injured by the guardian of the child;

(g) the guardian of the child is unable or unwilling to protect the child from emotional injury;

(h) the guardian of the child has subjected the child to or is unable or unwilling to protect the child from cruel and unusual treatment or punishment.

(i) repealed 2003 c16 s3.

(2.1) For the purposes of subsection (2)(c), a child is neglected if the guardian

(a) is unable or unwilling to provide the child with the necessities of life,

(b) is unable or unwilling to obtain for the child, or to permit the child to receive, essential medical, surgical or other remedial treatment that is necessary for the health or well-being of the child, or

(c) is unable or unwilling to provide the child with adequate care or supervision.

(3) For the purposes of this Act,

(a) a child is emotionally injured

(i) if there is impairment of the child's mental or emotional functioning or development, and

(ii) if there are reasonable and probable grounds to believe that the emotional injury is the result of

(A) rejection,

(A.1) emotional, social, cognitive or physiological neglect,

(B) deprivation of affection or cognitive stimulation,

(C) exposure to family violence or severe domestic disharmony,

(D) inappropriate criticism, threats, humiliation, accusations or expectations of or toward the child,

(E) the mental or emotional condition of the guardian of the child or of anyone living in the same residence as the child;